'Tis the Season

A collection of Christmas stories, poems and fun activities for you

by Sally Harper and Jackie Skipp

Tight Christmas

I'm dreaming of a tight Christmas.
Not like the ones I used to know,
Now the champagne's missing,
The turkey's chicken,
The booze is bulk-bought from Costco.

I'm dreaming of a tight Christmas.
I've cancelled Disney Plus and Sky,
Now the kids are whingeing
As I sit bingeing
On last year's long-expired mince pies.

I'm dreaming of a tight Christmas.
Recycled Auntie Mabel's gift.
Now the scented hankies
Are Auntie Annie's
I hope this won't start a family rift...

I'm dreaming of a tight Christmas.
I'm hoping Santa will be kind:
Refund my stocking
With cash for shopping
And pay November's parking fine...

I'm dreaming of a tight Christmas.
Playing Charades because it's cheap.
I'm no party pooper
In my drunken stupor,
Can't get that you're not supposed to speak.

I'm dreaming of a tight Christmas,
With every Christmas cheque I write.
May your bills be healthy and light!
And may all your Christmases be slight.

Sally

Valley of Hope

"Thank you for all your help!" The bus driver scowled at her and Judi felt glad that he had recognised the heavy sarcasm she had laced her words with. All she had asked for was a little bit of advice on the best ticket to buy, but he had been rude and impatient. She hoped everyone else in Wales was friendlier than him. She stumbled along the busy bus, trying to manoeuvre her little case past feet and shopping bags sticking out en-route. There was only one seat left and she could see why: in reality it was half a seat, the other half taken up by a large man in grubby work clothes. He was glaring at a child who was kneeling on the seat in front to stare at him.

"You're fat!" the little girl said provocatively and his scowl deepened as he reddened. Then the child's face disappeared, as she was hurriedly pulled down by an unknown hand that Judi identified as being elderly and female. Looking away, Judi perched sideways on the edge of the seat, her feet and case protruding into the gangway ready to trip the next unsuspecting passenger.

The man closed his eyes as the bus wound its way slowly along narrow, twisting roads, shiny with ice, that led through a succession of little villages. As Judi gazed at the snow-capped mountain looming in the background, a commotion arose in the seat in front.

"I don't want to go." The little girl screamed petulantly.

"Daddy is really looking forward to seeing you, darling."

"I don't like daddy and I don't like you!" The child kicked the seat in front.

The woman flicked open a large hardback book in an attempt to distract her. "Rosie, look at Nanny's book. See the sheep. There's lots of sheep around here too, look."

Rosie was having none of it. "It's a stupid book." A thud followed and Judi watched as the woman bent to retrieve the book from the floor, wincing painfully as she did. The little girl turned away and began to snivel, her face pressed against the window. Aberorton came into view, an unimpressive little village comprising rows of back-to-back houses flanking the disused pithead. Gingerly, the woman tapped the child's arm. "This is our stop, Rosie. Look out for Daddy."

"I don't want to go." This time the voice was pitiful, and Judi felt sure the plea was rooted in fear. As the bus stop came into view, she saw the solitary man beside it, wearing a distinctive red postman's coat. The grandmother was trying to manhandle the little girl down the aisle, and the man looked anxious as he stepped forward, ready to help them off.

Judi watched as the doors opened and he greeted the little girl who pulled back, hiding behind her grandmother who glanced apprehensively at the driver and said "Diolche drive." Looking hurt, the man pulled two cases from the luggage rack at the front of the bus and deposited them on the road before reaching back up to help the woman down the step. The bus started up and as it rumbled on past them,

Judi saw the man pick up the little girl who kicked and screamed, her breath visible in the cold air. The woman stroked her back, in an attempt to calm her. It was a sad sight.

Judi slipped quickly into the seat in front before the bus picked up speed, and then she saw it. The book lay on the floor, under the window. As she reached for it, she could see it was quite an old book, which must have been expensive in its day. The shiny veneer of its hardback cover was still pristine. Flicking through it, she was surprised to see the pages were all intact and clean; there were no scribbles or finger-marks. Illustrated in bright colours, it told the story of a young girl and her animal friends on vacation around the world with the animals all kitted out in the national dress of each country they visited. On the inside of the front cover, she saw that the book had been published in 1965, and above the date was an inscription: "To Naeve, these will be my adventures. One day they can be yours too. All my love, Ralph. 20th October 1966."

She looked up from the book to see her stop ahead and hurriedly rang the bell. As she got off, she tried to give the book to the driver.

He regarded her coldly. "Stick it on the luggage rack and I'll hand it in later."

A young woman behind her spoke close to her ear. "He'll throw it in the bin more like, miserable old devil."

Judi looked at the man and decided the woman was probably right. She tucked the book under her arm and stepped off the bus, without a clue about what she intended to do with it, only that she wasn't going to leave it with him.

Trudging down the street, she tried to switch her mind away from brightly coloured books and frightened children. She had an interview in 25 minutes at Abernock Animal Sanctuary and she had to find the place yet. This was a big step for her, having lived in London all her life, and it terrified her. But then, leaving Ian after six years had terrified her, yet she'd done it and survived. It had made her re-evaluate her life, and she'd realised her work life was dull and unfulfilling and her social life – well, that was virtually non-existent. And so, she had made the brave decision to seek a fresh start and the proverbial pastures anew.

The receptionist at the Sanctuary greeted her warmly when she arrived and happily agreed to look after her case during the interview. Whatever the outcome, Judi had decided that a trip to Wales so close to Christmas definitely merited sticking around for a couple of days to explore the area.   Dropping into a battered fabric tub chair, she took deep breaths to calm her nerves, and mentally rehearsed questions and responses she had thought of earlier.

"They're ready for you now. Good luck."   The receptionist gave her a double thumbs up.

Judi smiled nervously at the panel of three when she entered the room. The two men rose, the woman merely waved, her phone to her ear. She was dressed informally in jeans and sweatshirt and her hands were streaked with mud. "Yes, I'll hold!" she barked into the phone.

"I'm Gwynne Jones, Chairman of the Trustees." the younger of the two men told Judi, formally offering his hand. "Thank you for attending."

The second man smiled warmly. "I'm Tom – and this very busy lady next to me is Bethan, our Centre Manager. Is this the first time you've visited our valleys?"

Judi nodded. "Yes."

"Well, you're very welcome here." He indicated for her to sit in a chair ready for interrogation. As she lowered herself, she realised to her horror that she still had the book tucked under her arm.

Gwynne's eyes followed hers and he regarded her quizzically. "Does the book have a relevance to this interview?"

Oh well, Judi thought, it could be an icebreaker. She told her story and flicked open the pages so they could see. "It's lovely, isn't it?" She put on her brightest smile for them all.

9

Gwynne was unimpressed. "Do you feel that books portraying animals wearing clothes are appropriate, Miss Whiting?" he asked. She saw Tom wince, and Bethan, who was still holding on the phone, shook her head and exhaled deliberately.

"I'm sure we have more relevant things to ask". She turned to Judi. "Can you tell us more about your admin experience?" Bethan had got her off the hook.

Judi recounted details of her eight years in various admin posts, directing smiles between the three panel members. Only Tom smiled back. Gwynne remained unrelentingly straight-faced and Bethan began listening again to the voice at the end of the phone. By the time Tom asked her about her work with her local Dogs' Home, Bethan had finished her call, but her mobile continued to beep, and her attention was torn between Judi and her incoming messages. Judi's nerve was leaving her by the minute as she hesitatingly described how she'd dog-walked and fundraised for her local rescue.

"So, you've got no paid experience of working in a rescue environment?" Gwynne raised his eyebrows as though surprised.

Judi opened her mouth to reply, but Tom beat her to it. "I feel volunteering is every bit as valuable as paid employment. And the post is admin-based, which Judi seems to be amply experienced in. Is that correct, Judi?"

Judi nodded and prepared herself for more questions. She was relieved when the interview was finally over and they thanked her for coming. As she left the room, Bethan called after her. "Oh, Judi. When would you be able to start – if you got the job?"

Judi felt deflated as she walked away from the Centre; despite Bethan's final question, she felt she'd done badly. The book was again firmly lodged under her arm, and she wondered how on earth she was going to track down its owner. She decided her first step should be to return to Aberorton where Rosie and her grandmother had got off.

The bus passed a pub as it pulled in towards the stop, giving Judi inspiration. Where better to start than the village local? Besides, it was two o' clock and she hadn't had lunch yet. She glanced around the pub as she entered the bar, dismayed to see it was virtually empty. The young barmaid greeted her pleasantly and as Judi ordered half a lager and dropped the book onto the bar while she delved in her bag for her purse, she tipped her head to one side and glanced at the shiny cover through her jet-black fringe. "Cool book". She nodded to emphasise her words.

Judi sighed. "I'm trying to find its owner." She recounted the tale to the girl who listened patiently and thoughtfully.

"Maud's your best bet." She inclined her head towards an elderly lady sitting alone reading a newspaper, half a Guinness in her hand. "She knows everything about everyone in this village." She shouted across the bar "Maud, do you know a lady with a grand-daughter called Rosie, whose dad's a postie? This lady's trying to get this book back to her."

Maud looked across brightly at them. "That'll be Moira Evans and her son Danny. They live in Bennett Street. No. 9, I think, but I wouldn't be sure." Judi sat down with her drink at the next table to Maud, and the little woman eyed her enthusiastically before continuing, "The family moved here from Aberfan years ago, but Moira moved in with Danny when his marriage broke up. Heartbroken, he was." Maud fell silent for a moment, then shook her head. "Moira's a nice woman, but she has a sadness about her sometimes. Like everyone from Aberfan, the sorrow lingers, even all these years later."

"Why is she sad?" Judi asked and Maud pursed her lips, shaking her head again. "Maybe you're too young to know, but you should look it up. Everyone should know. It was a terrible thing that happened in Aberfan."

The door opened and Maud's expression changed as she turned to wave to a woman who looked like a larger, younger version of her. "My daughter." She explained to Judi as she folded away the newspaper.

Judi thanked Maud for her help and returned to the bar to order food before taking up a window seat where she looked up Aberfan. She gasped as she began to read about the horrors of that day; her heart lurched at the grainy images of the tiny school covered in blackness and tears filled her eyes reading the accounts of the desperate human chain of villagers who toiled tirelessly to try to save their children.

During the short walk from the pub to Bennett Street, the story and images weighed heavily on her. In her bag was the sandwich from the pub. She had wrapped it in a napkin, her appetite gone. She took a deep breath as she turned the corner into the street and found no. 9, hoping Maud had been right. She rang the bell and was greeted with a high-pitched incessant yapping which she guessed came from a small dog. Sure enough, as the woman she recognised instantly from the bus answered the door, a little Jack Russell terrier scuttled away from her.

Moira smiled. "He's all talk until I open the door, then he's scared to death." The dog had stopped at the end of the passageway and was cautiously inching his way back towards Judi. She crouched down, offering her hand to him, and he sniffed her warily before licking her hand and allowing her to fuss him.

Moira's mouth dropped open. "Well, I've never known him be that brave. It usually takes him ages to trust people. He was abused in his last home."

It was a story Judi had heard many times, and it always made her angry, but she remembered why she was here and straightened up, pulling the book out from under her arm. "You dropped this on the bus. I didn't want to just hand it in." She suddenly felt silly and added "In case it didn't get back to you."

She didn't expect the reaction she got. Moira's hand flew to her face and tears filled her eyes. "Duw Duw!! Oh, thank goodness! Ralph! Ralph! The book's been found." She gestured to Judi, "Oh, do come in, please!"

Judi followed her along the passage uncertainly, the dog trotting along beside her. As she entered a small lounge, a very elderly man attempted to push himself up from a settee to greet her.

"No, Ralph, stay there." Moira put a hand on his shoulder and turned to Judi. "This is my brother, Ralph." She flapped at the little dog. "Pippin, leave the lady alone – I'm sorry, what was your name?"

"Judi. I was sitting behind you on the bus."

Moira looked shamefaced. "I do apologise if Rosie disturbed you."

"The child's unsettled, doesn't know what's been going on." Ralph's voice was surprisingly strong but as he turned towards her, she started momentarily at the depth of cloudiness in his eyes. He smiled weakly. "Thank you so much, this book means a great deal to our family."

"Rosie has been living in Chepstow for almost a year with her mother, Ellen." Moira told Judi. "Ellen's mother has been terminally ill for a long time and it put pressure on my son's marriage." She sighed. "Thankfully, they've resolved things, but Ellen's mum has only days to live. I've brought Rosie back so Ellen can spend her time at the Hospice, before she comes back to us."

It was a bittersweet story. "Where's Rosie now?" Judi asked.

Moira smiled. "Down the park with her dad. It's amazing how quickly five-year-olds come round."

There was a moment's silence, and Judi glanced at the book, which Moira was hugging close to her chest. "It's a beautiful book." she said. "So well looked after for its age."

"It's one of my most precious possessions." Moira glanced at Ralph. "It was a gift from Ralph to my twin sister Naeve. The day he left Aberfan to join the RAF, he gave us both beautiful books to remind us that life was an adventure for us all to enjoy. We were eight at the time." Moira sat down, waving a hand weakly towards Judi, suggesting she sat too. Ralph patted her hand and she took a deep breath before continuing.

"It was the day before the Aberfan disaster. My book was very special to me, because it came from Ralph, but I was never a great reader – but Naeve, she read her book from cover to cover that day. She read the last two chapters with a torch in bed, she loved it so much. She told me all about it the next morning – and given half a chance, she'd have stayed in bed all day and read it again." Moira's eyes began to well up again. "I didn't go to school the next day. I had a rash so me mam kept me home, but Naeve went off as usual." She wiped at her face with the back of her hand. "I'm sorry, Judi. I always get emotional talking about it. She never came back. And I've kept her book all these years. I was devastated when I thought I'd lost it."

"I'm so sorry." It was a whisper, and it was all Judi could think of to say. Ralph was gazing sadly at the carpet. Even Pippin sat quietly now, as though aware of the mood in the room. Then to her horror, her phone rang.

"Answer your phone, dear. It's fine." Moira smiled kindly through her tears.

As Judi put the phone to her ear, Bethan, the Rescue Centre Manager began to speak. As before, she was to the point, but her tone was friendly. She apologised for being distracted during the interview – she had been dealing with an urgent situation, trying to get a dog out of a pound before it was put to sleep. "Anyway, that's how I am. If you think you can put up with me, I'd love to offer you the job." she concluded.

Judi didn't have to think twice. If there was a lesson about taking your chances in life whenever they came up, she had just learned it.

Judi said goodbye to Ralph and Moira walked her to the door, with Pippin at her heels. "If you are going to be working in Abernock, there's a very good bus service there from here – even if one of the drivers is a bit miserable." Moira told her with a wink. "Accommodation is a bit cheaper here, and I'm sure Pippin would love to take you for a few walks with me."

"I'd love that." On impulse, Judi turned and embraced Moira. They heard a shriek of laughter and turned to see Danny jogging down the street with Rosie bumping up and down on his shoulders. It had begun to snow and their hairs were white with flakes. It felt as though this little valley was full of hope.

Jackie

Elfish Behaviour

"Oi!"

The shout ricochet off the machinery and for a moment, everything seemed to pause, even the voice-boxes in the Mechanical Doll area silenced themselves.

Aubrey's shoulders tensed and his stomach lurched.

"That's the second time this morning you've left your workbench!"

Aubrey sighed and clutched the letter stuffed inside his pocket. Would he never make it past the first paragraph? Bloody Bodkin was too sharp for his own good. He must have thought all his Christmases had come at once the day he was made Shop Floor Supervisor (Wooden Toys and Puppets Division).

Bodkin's eyes narrowed, highlighting his cute button nose and rosy cheeks. "What's that?" He jabbed a pointy finger at Aubrey's tights. "In your pocket?"

When this had happened last month, Aubrey remembered, his Union Rep had told him he didn't have to answer. In fact, he recalled, it was better not to say anything at all until he had representation. Bodkin had hated that meeting, had been gunning for him ever since. Every tiny little misdemeanour – accidentally hammering a batch of Jack-in-a Boxes shut, miscalculating the scale of the mice in the Noah's Ark collection so they all came out the same size as the elephants, fitting a few wonky wheels to the dogs on strings – every error was gleefully recorded by Bodkin in his nasty little notebook. He stared at the floor with grim concentration, counting seventeen identical brass-buckled green shoes beneath seventeen identical workbenches. The eighteenth was his.

"I said ..." began Bodkin. But he was cut off by a screaming claxon.

"Sir! Sir! Quick! There's been an accident!" yelled someone from the Spinning Top Department.

Aubrey didn't look up until he was sure Bodkin had gone, whisked away in panic. He thought he heard the words: "spring too tight" and "emergency surgery" but couldn't be sure. He shuddered at the thought. Some poor bugger was in for the chop then, one way or the other. Santa was notorious for sacking the injured and maimed; anything to avoid paying out on the insurance. That Union Rep was in for another busy season.

With the drama elsewhere, he took his opportunity and ran up the stairs to the toilet. Letters from his cousin Jonty always had to be read as quickly as possible. Ever since Jonty had escaped factory life and fled to the Dark Side, he'd become unpredictable and dangerously spontaneous. Two letters ago, just as Aubrey read the line "I'll be paying you a visit very soon," Jonty had leapt up behind and pulled his hat off, screaming "Always watch your back, Cuz!"

Working for the Dark Side, it seemed to Aubrey, certainly had its attractions. Despite the permanent damage to his reputation and his newly acquired place on Santa's Hit List (officially the Naughty List), in the past year Jonty was the richest he'd ever been and had barely worked a day. Occasionally he'd refer to his mysterious "Training Days" and disappear for several weeks, emerging with fresh bruises, new muscles and a hint of evil in his cheeky eyes. Aubrey knew not to ask questions. All the factory elves did. Any hint of anything illegal like that and Bodkin would be all over them, ready to load his notebook with incriminating details and shoot them all down.

Jonty's handwriting had always been terrible. It took several attempts before Aubrey realised that the letter b was really an h and the number 5 was vaguely trying to be an e:

Alright, Cuz? it said, *Still one of Santa's slaves? Don't know how you stick it. Glad I didn't. Anyway, me and the lads have got a vacancy and wondered if you'd like to break out and taste a bit of the high-life? You'll get four times the wage that bearded dictator gives you and only have to work 24 days a year! Not bad eh?*

Aubrey's hands were sweaty; his fingers were smudging the ink. He felt his conscious screaming inside him: *Say no to temptation! Remember what Mother always said about Jonty, that he's a bad one, no better than a common imp! Just like his father....*

His throat was dry as a box of stuffing and his heart hammered like a tin drum set but he had to keep reading.

... Anyway, you know I can't tell you more until I see you face-to-face so keep this hush-hush, won't you?

That confirmed it. This smelt highly illegal. And dangerous. Aubrey swallowed again (and oddly, tasted marshmallows). The cistern dripped and wheezed behind him; fighting the pointless battle with its near-frozen pipes. It sounded like Bodkin. For a horrifying moment, he pictured himself as old and defeated by factory life as Bodkin, his hat dented, his green suit stained and sickly – the only highlight of his life a new notebook when the old one was full of spiteful tell-tales. His eyes drank in more of Jonty's scrawl:

... so for once in your life, Cuz, grow a pair and get out of that rut you're in. Basically, we're a man down. Some bad stuff went down on the 22nd and we need a replacement. Meet me on Christmas Eve (there was a barely legible address) and I'll tell you what to do. Bring a change of elf-suit, a spare hat and make sure no-one follows you. You won't regret it!

Jonty

And now somehow here he was, in a far from salubrious tree house dive of a tavern somewhere too close to the Human border for comfort. In an effort to avoid eye-contact with the gang of goblins shouting at the bar, he studied his glass of moonshine and wondered again if it was supposed to be luminous yellow. Jonty sat opposite on a small stool that ridiculed his muscular, tattooed frame but would have fitted Aubrey perfectly. He was in the process of lighting a pipe but the spark from his candy cane lighter wouldn't take.

26

Every swear word he muttered made Aubrey's rosy cheeks flush an even deeper pink and he could feel the goblins' scarlet pupils boring into him every time he spoke. Had he always sounded so effeminate?

"Baubles!" swore Jonty again and flung the pipe to the floor. He leaned forward and lowered his voice so Aubrey had to strain his pointed ears to catch what he said. He'd had three Moonshines for each one of Aubrey's so his words were as thick as syrup.

"You've probably heard nothing but lies about us," said Jonty. "I know what the factory folk think." He pointed a bitten fingernail at Aubrey. "You think we're all murderous layabouts, don't you? Wreaking havoc night after night, breaking in, stealing, vandalism..."

"No, no," said Aubrey too quickly. "Far from it."

In the foreground, Jonty glared at him. In the background, the biggest goblin leered at him and licked his warty lips. If he didn't leave in the next two minutes, he'd be elf-meat.

"If I agree to start work tomorrow," said Aubrey boldly, "Can we go?"

Jonty downed his glass, grinned and turned round to face the goblins. "Cheers, Steve! I owe you a pint for that!"

The biggest goblin raised his glass and winked at Aubrey. "No problem Jonty, mate," he said, "Nothing a little bit of Goblin pressure can't do." He blew a kiss at Aubrey and the whole gang laughed. Aubrey had never been so glad to leave somewhere.

After an uncomfortable night in a cave that Jonty said used to belong to a herd of rebel unicorns (to be fair, he had tried to shovel up the worst of the poo), they roasted some acorns on a portable stove and set out for the border. Jonty gave him a satchel with some documents in it. "Show the guards this and keep your mouth shut, alright? I'll do the talking."

Aubrey nodded and tried to keep his breakfast down. He remembered his cosy little workbench and tools, his company hot-chocolate mug and company hat and sighed.

What must Bodkin be thinking? Elves were never ill, especially not with Gnomonia. And never on the busiest night of the year. Hopefully the Christmas Eve sleigh-loading frenzy would distract him.

The ogres on duty looked fat and bored. They lowered their pistols and barely raised an eye as Jonty and Aubrey walked past. Aubrey noticed a warehouse straight after the border. A door had been left open, the dim light illuminating hundreds of decimated advent calendars.

"They loot them," whispered Jonty.

"Happens every year. They steal all the chocolates and gorge on them. They've all got bellyache now. That's why they can't be bothered with the likes of us. Don't even ask what happened to the poor buggers who tried to smuggle them through." He winked. "Let's just say it led to more bellyache...."

Aubrey couldn't conceal his horror. "You mean they opened all the windows *at once*? Even the last one?"

Jonty laughed but there was no warmth behind it. "Well, the last door's the best one, isn't it? Biggest chocolate. "He shook his head but it didn't jangle. The bell on the top of his hat was missing. "That's nothing, you'll soon learn. Can't believe how green you are Cuz."

Aubrey still couldn't believe how it was possible to be so high up but to have fallen so low. He glanced at his cousin and wondered how he could do such terrible things. The clock on the mantelpiece in the humans' living room had long ticked past eleven and the pale December morning light was struggling to break through the curtains. He felt sick. Santa would be here soon. The devastation was everywhere.

When Jonty had first told him to rip all the baubles off the beautiful Christmas tree, he'd thought it was joke. But then Aubrey had said, "Not that like that, you soft jellybaby, put some bloody effort into it. It's Christmas Eve! The big finale! Look, like this!"

He tore into the defenceless fir like a butcher, stripping it of its shiny glass baubles and smashing them on the floor. Jonty's eyes gleamed. "Go on then, Cuz!" He yelled, "Grind it in. Like this!" He jumped up and down on the fragments, crunching the shards deep into the carpet. Before he knew what he was doing, a terrible rush of euphoria grabbed Aubrey and he did the same, stamping and laughing in a voice that didn't sound like his own.

"That's it! More!" egged on Jonty.

Aubrey jumped up and down on the maimed baubles, possessed with the exhilaration of his new found freedom. He could feel the jagged glass piercing through the soles of his slippers and shredding the soles of his feet but he danced on regardless, enjoying the way the blood stained the cream rug under the radiator.

Jonty screamed in ecstasy as he pulled the entire tree down. It crashed to the floor with a moan. Jonty tugged at Aubrey's arm and suddenly he was submerged in its horizontal branches, copying his cousin who ripped and sliced at the poor thing's trunk with what looked like a miniature chainsaw. Within minutes, the tree was a pile of firewood on a multi-coloured mat of broken glass.

They lay panting on their backs. Jonty's pointed ears and rosy cheeks glowed with pleasure. "Wow Cuz," he said, "That was great. Proper destruction job. I'm proud of you. More of that tomorrow, yeah?"

But Aubrey couldn't share his glee. His high had nose-dived into a sucking pit of guilt. What had he done? He pictured Santa, Bodkin, all his old factory mates. All of them shaking their heads in disappointment and something far worse. Sadness. Genuine sadness that he'd been so weak and had been so eager to crush the first sparks of true Christmas spirit. The same Christmas spirit they'd all worked so hard to achieve since January. He'd never forgive himself.

"Right, then. Job's not finished yet. Now for the *acting*!" Jonty hauled him up to his bleeding feet. "No self-respecting Elf-on-the-Shelf leaves it like this." He stretched, flexing his muscular frame and Aubrey noticed for the first time how short he was. And how squeaky his voice was. And how pathetic.

By the time Jonty had finished positioning himself in a cheeky pose in front of the ruins, holding the chainsaw at a whimsical angle, Aubrey had fled from the house.

By the time the human screams of horror filtered from the living-room, through the front door and out into the chill of the winter street, he was flying determinedly back to the North Pole.

And by the time he'd arrived at work, where Bodkin bathed and bandaged his feet and an exhausted and extremely grumpy Santa had issued him a warning for tardiness, he knew he'd made the right decision.

He'd apply for Union Rep in the New Year.

Sally

A Gift of Love

As I stood on the banks of my local river, I heard the shuffling sound behind me, and out of the wooded area I had walked through appeared a very elderly lady. I glanced at her curiously; she was tall and broad and wore layers of cloth in different hues of blue and brown and green, which hung untidily and made her look as though she were wearing a rag-bag. She smiled as she stopped beside me but as we stood together, her expression changed. She looked tired and dispirited, but she also looked angry.

I attempted conversation. "Are you taking time out from the Christmas Eve rush like me?"

Ignoring my question, she asked me "Are you a mother?"

"Yes," I replied

"So am I. Sometimes I wish I wasn't." I looked at her, thinking that was an awful thing to say, but I saw a tear roll down her face, and more than that, I felt a dreadful endless sadness emanate from her. I had no idea what to say and so I stood in silence with her and watched as a plastic bag floated down the river, snagging on a twig as it did.

Eventually she spoke again. "What will you give your children for Christmas this year?"

The question took me by surprise. I had bought my three children a lot. I hesitantly began to tell her about the computer games, the mobile phone, the clothes, the pamper sets and cosmetics...

As I spoke, the plastic bag freed itself, sailing quickly past me. With an unimaginable deftness and lack of fear, she leaned quickly out to snatch the bag from the fast-running water and held it between her large, weathered hands, scrunching it up. Shocked, I stopped talking. I had the feeling she had stopped listening to my list, anyway.

"I gave all my children the most wonderful present. It was like an enormous blanket of many colours and textures. It gave them everything they could ever need." She turned to face me and I realised that her skin was ancient but young all at once, with not a single line on her face. She studied me unnervingly and I noticed her huge chest was heaving with emotion. "But my children didn't care about my gift of love, they have destroyed great parts of it and they keep on doing it."

She was silent for a moment but when she spoke again, I heard her regret. "And I am guilty, I have caused destruction too - my fires and floods wreaked havoc on my own gift. I did it through anger but I wanted to show all my children what would happen if they didn't appreciate and look after my gift."

My heart was beating fast as recognition began to dawn on who the elderly woman could be. But was that even possible?

She looked at me again. "I think there is hope for my beautiful gift to recover but it needs the help of people like you." For the first time, I noticed the strange green light in her eyes. She reached out to touch my arm and there was a warmth in her hand which didn't belong in this cold, frosty day "Do what you can – and always remember, the little things matter. Lift the plastic bag off the tree before it is swept into the river." She smiled kindly as my cheeks burned slightly. "Do what you can, and let your voice be heard – speak out for Nature. And most importantly, teach your children to do the same."

I nodded – and meant it. And I watched as Mother Earth turned and walked back through her woods to wherever she needed to go next.

Jackie

Christmas Massacre

No-one saw Lucy leave the house. Its gleaming letter box and sumptuous holly wreath hid the devastation inside so well it was as if they'd been trained to do so.

Inside, the chessboard floor tiles in the hallway seemed untouched, indeed every painting on the walls – the faded landscapes and pet portraits - the perfectly aligned Christmas cards strung across the wall with charming scenes of ice skaters and mangers remained in position. Somehow, despite all that had occurred, the mirror by the coat stand had not cracked; the vase of mistletoe stayed intact. The sitting room also gave little away – the furniture orderly and well-matched with no blood visible.

The pile of limbs and other assorted body parts in the kitchen, therefore, was a shock. A tangle of flesh and fibre, it was hard to tell how many had been butchered. None had survived. A hand here, a foot there, the corpses hugged each other in a petrified embrace. Legs had been broken and bent back into unnatural angles; noses smashed; clothes torn and ripped; several bodies naked. Pots and pans, spilling roast potatoes and gravy lay scattered in a violet trail of rage through to the dining room where yet more bodies lay amongst the shredded Christmas crackers.

Here the furniture had also been violated, a graceful table of the finest oak lay marooned on its back, legs splayed and broken on a sea of smashed china. An upended sugar bowl mourned its scattered cubes and spoon on the other side of the fireplace. A nativity scene was nothing but fragments, the baby Jesus had lost its head. The house was a shrine to violence: a frozen scene of terror and misery.

The revenge continued its ruin up the stairs where beds morphed into coffins and the bath cradled a sickening mix of dismembered heads and bare torsos. The house wept. All was lost, all was gone. Years of happy times and laughter, Christmases past, present and now future, all crushed and ripped away from the foundations to the chimney pots.

Cruelly, the sun shone the next day. Before inspecting the contents of her stocking tied to the end of the bed, Amanda felt her way through the darkness to open up her beloved dolls' house. Had Santa been?

In the next bedroom, Lucy heard her sister's scream and smirked.

He certainly had.

Sally

The Opportunity

Something about the gentle consistency of her old trainers padding along the muddy towpath always gave Fiona a welcome sense of calm. The past few months hadn't been easy, with the stresses of work and James' leaving, but she'd come to realise that sometimes the simplest pleasures were the best cure. Meg bounded ahead, her tail swinging side to side like a rudder, pausing every few feet to sniff at the long grass by the water's edge. Fiona shivered in the December light, pulling her jacket tight around her middle to keep out the biting wind. The zip had broken weeks ago and she hadn't had the energy or inclination to buy a new one, let alone the funds. She also couldn't face buying the next size up - since Ed had gone, chocolate digestives and takeaways had become her staple diet. And now Christmas had arrived along with the Christmas hamper she'd ordered in better times, adding its temptations of chocolates, cheeses and wine. Even thinking about the hours of solitary gluttony that lay ahead made her blush and avert her eyes, even with nobody around to avert them from.

Weak sunshine struggled to break through the overcast sky as Fiona crossed the bridge. She thought of the hectic scenes playing over and over in the estate behind her as kids opened their presents and parents watched with bleary eyes and cups of tea. The only activity here came courtesy of a handful of mallards bickering at the lock gates. A few narrow boats bobbed up and down in the murky canal. There was a sorry-looking string of tinsel in the window of the *Lucky Jim*, its redness highlighting the grime of the curtains behind it. *Yes*, she thought, unable to help herself. *Lucky, lucky Jim with his flashy new job, shiny new flat and sparkling new girlfriend.*

The boats neighbours: *Kestrel* and *Swan Lake* seemed to be permanent residents; their inhabitants living secret lives behind portholes. What would it be like to live in a boat instead of a house? Romantic notions of cosy wood burners and feeding ducks through the portholes filled her mind. There was something very appealing about perching at the front of a boat with a steaming mug of tea and a bacon sandwich, throwing crumbs to passing swans - before setting off and moving lazily downstream to who-knew-where.

Meg's bark broke her daydream. The collie was circling frantically on the bank, pouncing at something out of sight in the reeds. Fiona ran over - Meg had an unfortunate fondness for water voles.

"All right, Meg, I'm coming, what is it?"

"It's my rope!" called a male voice.

Fiona stopped. A tatty narrowboat, the *Opportunity,* was floating adrift in the middle of the canal. A man with curly brown hair and a scruffy beard stood at the back, and to Fiona's mind, dressed rather inappropriately for winter, in a pair of old khaki shorts and a thin T-shirt. One of his feet was perched on the edge of the boat, the fingertips of his left hand stretched so far they could barely grip the rudder. The wind was forcing the whole boat away from the bank and it was now almost horizontal - a floating barrier blocking the whole canal. The man waved at her, his smile anxious.

"Can you give me a hand?" he yelled, barely audible over Meg's barking. "I was pulling her in but the wind blew us back and the rope can't reach!"

Fiona tried to hide the rising panic pulsing through her. James had always made a point of telling her how clumsy and impractical she was. She hesitated before walking gingerly to the very edge of the canal bank. Thick, grey water swirled beneath.

"Can you see the rope?" asked the man, his words almost lost in the wind, but all she could see was grass and mud. Meg barked and pounced again until Fiona found the thick coiled rope, nestling in the undergrowth like a snake.

"I've got it!" she yelled, grabbing it before it could slither back into the depths of the canal. But before she could ask the bearded man what to do next she heard a ferocious bark. Another dog, much bigger than Meg, burst out of the boat's back doors and leapt into the canal with an enormous splash.

"Tucker, no!" shouted the man, but the huge animal was already clambering out and shaking itself dry on the bank, growling so fiercely at Meg that she shrank back to Fiona's side, whimpering.

"Sorry! Don't worry, his bark is worse than his bite, literally - he's had most of his teeth removed," called the man who had now drifted so far back he was in danger of entangling himself in the bushes on the opposite side. "Can you grab him for me?"

Fiona glanced around but there was no-one else to help. With one swift move she grabbed the dog by the collar, who was so surprised at such a firm intervention he immediately whimpered and lay down at her feet.

"Wow, well done!" she heard the man shout.

Tucker dealt with, Fiona held up the rope again. "What shall I do with...?" she started, but the man was looking nervously over towards the locks. A smart narrowboat was merrily chugging its way out of the gates, a transistor belting out carols strapped to the roof – and it was heading straight towards the stranded *Opportunity*.

"Quick!" he instructed, "Plant your feet into the ground, tie the rope around your waist and try to pull us across. It's easier if you lean back."

Her heart thudding like a bass drum, Fiona followed his instructions. She was relieved to find that there was more than enough rope to circle her middle, despite her fears. It occurred to her that for once her sturdiness was a positive thing, allowing her to ease the boat towards the bank without being dragged into the canal.

Just in time, they moored the *Opportunity* safely, allowing the other boat to sail past, its occupants smilingly raising plastic champagne flutes in amusement at the sideshow. Fiona realised the man was beside her on the bank now, heaving a sigh of relief as he finished knotting the rope into place. He smiled at her and it was only then she noticed how handsome he was.

"Thanks for that!" he said, his voice warm with gratitude. "I've only had her for six months. I suppose I'm still learning the ropes. Sorry, terrible pun not intended," he apologised with a grin. Fiona couldn't help laughing, aware as she did so how long it had been since she'd even smiled. She'd almost forgotten how good it felt. The man held out a hand.

"I'm Tom, by the way."

She shook it and now she was blushing again, but this time with happiness, not shame.

"Fiona." She looked directly into his eyes and smiled again.

"I suppose I didn't realise that living on a boat isn't as easy as it looks," continued Tom. "I was so naive I honestly thought it would be endless hot breakfasts outside in the sunny mornings, followed by cruising down the canal to

wherever I happened to fancy going that day."
He reached down and patted Tucker who had
fallen asleep next to Meg on the grass. "Nobody
tells you about the maintenance, the mooring
fees, the weather, emptying the toilets. Or the
bloody winter!" He shook his head and
shrugged happily. "Still, I wouldn't change it
for the world."

Heavy clouds loomed overhead and Fiona
shivered. Drawing her broken jacket around
herself, she reluctantly decided it was time to
move on.

"Well, I'm glad to be of service. Come on Meg,
time to go home."

But Meg refused to move.

Tom's anxious expression returned briefly.
"Wait, you look cold. Er, do you fancy some
tea? I've got a box of mince pies somewhere. Or
maybe some digestives if they're not your
thing? No chocolate ones though I'm afraid,
they only had the boring ones left in the shop."
He seemed as nervous as she was. "We could sit

here, at the back, watch the wildlife? It's more sheltered onboard. It's the least I can do!"

With a shy smile, Fiona nodded and as she saw Tom's face light up, she realised it was indeed time to move on, in a different sense. His green eyes were bright even as the cloud dimmed the sunlight.

He held out his hand. It was warm. "Great! Then, please, step aboard! Oh, and Merry Christmas by the way!"

She smiled again. It felt good. "Merry Christmas!"

Sally

A Peckham Christmas

On the First Day of Christmas, my true love gave to me a dodgy colour TV

On the Second Day of Christmas, my true love gave to me two blow up dolls, and a dodgy colour TV

On the Third Day of Christmas, my true love gave to me three moulting wigs, two blow up dolls and a dodgy colour TV

On the Fourth Day of Christmas, my true love gave to me four crash turbans, three moulting wigs, two blow up dolls and a dodgy colour TV

On the Fifth Day of Christmas, my true love gave to me five Chan-de-liers, four crash turbans, three moulting wigs, two blow up dolls and a dodgy colour TV

On the Sixth Day of Christmas, my true love gave to me six batman costumes, five Chan-de-liers, four crash turbans, three moulting wigs, two blow up dolls and a dodgy colour TV

On the Seventh Day of Christmas, my true love gave to me seven tins of green paint, six batman costumes, five Chan-de-liers, four crash turbans, three moulting wigs, two blow up dolls and a dodgy colour TV

On the Eighth Day of Christmas, my true love gave to me eight mobile phones, seven tins of green paint, six batman costumes, five Chan-de-liers, four crash turbans, three moulting wigs, two blow up dolls and a dodgy colour TV

On the Ninth Day of Christmas, my true love gave to me nine Filofaxes, eight mobile phones, seven tins of green paint, six batman costumes, five Chan-de-liers, four crash turbans, three moulting wigs, two blow up dolls and a dodgy colour TV

On the Tenth Day of Christmas, my true love gave to me ten bottled waters, nine Filofaxes, eight mobile phones, seven tins of green paint, six batman costumes, five Chan-de-liers, four crash turbans, three moulting wigs, two blow up dolls and a dodgy colour TV

On the Eleventh Day of Christmas, my true love gave to me eleven Virgin Marys, ten bottled waters, nine Filofaxes, eight mobile phones, seven tins of green paint, six batman costumes, five Chan-de-liers, four crash turbans, three moulting wigs, two blow up dolls and a dodgy colour TV

On the Twelfth Day of Christmas, my true love gave to me ...Leave it out, Rodney, we'll have no stock left! You Plonker!!

Jackie

A Christmas Crisis

Shelley stared at the spindly artificial tree with contempt. It lay in its torn box next to a bag of cheap-looking baubles, obviously all straight from the charity shop. She studied her mother's message on her phone again. The battery was low. The battery was always low because her phone was so old but she had zilch chance of getting a new one for Christmas. She'd be lucky to get anything decent for Christmas.

Her mother ended her message with three kisses. She was working extra hours – that was becomingly a nightly occurrence just lately – she was sorry, but hoped Shelley had seen the tree and thought they could have a hot chocolate and decorate it together when she got in.

"Well, she can think again." Shelley muttered under her breath. She loved decorating the Christmas tree. When it was a proper tree that was, not some pathetic little reject. Shelley wandered into the kitchen and opened the fridge, her eyes searching the full shelves. Finding nothing that took her fancy, she slammed the door shut and opened the cupboard. Digestive biscuits, no thank you! Reaching into her pocket, she pulled out the letter about her school trip, the one she knew 'they wouldn't be able to afford'. Tearing it into pieces, she threw it down on the worktop "Damn the cost-of-living crisis." she announced to the room, before she ran up the stairs and threw herself down on her bed, where she allowed tears of frustration to run unchecked down her face.

"Someone's feeling a bit sorry fer 'erself." Shelley shot up on the bed to see a teenage girl swinging contentedly in her hanging egg chair. Her thick blonde hair curled and waved boldly around her thin face. She wore an old-fashioned woollen dress in a check print, with a white rounded collar and she watched Shelley with interest.

Shelley blinked hard and squeezed her eyes shut momentarily before rubbing them with her fists, as she shook her head. When she opened them, the girl gave a harsh laugh. "Yer not dreaming, I'm really here."

Swallowing hard, Shelley edged back up the bed, away from the figure. Her mouth opened to scream but the girl leant forward, urgently putting a finger to her lips and for reasons she couldn't explain, Shelley found herself obeying her. Instead, she asked shakily. "Who are you? W-what do you want?"

"Me name's Betty." Relaxing back in the chair again, Betty tipped her head to one side, studying Shelley quizzically. "What do I want? Well, I suppose you'd say I'm here to give you a reality check." She shrugged. "Now them's new words for me – we never said that back in the 30s and 40s. As Shelley stared at her uncomprehendingly, Betty added "When I grew up."

"What are you even talking about?" Shelley was aware of the thumping in her chest as she hissed the sentence.

Betty's gaze was steady. "I think you know. You may be a spoilt brat, but you're not stupid."

She looked around the room. "I died here – or at least in this space. It was an old house when I lived here."

"It still is." Whilst her brain pounded with the words "She's a ghost. You're talking to a ghost." perversely Shelley felt her fear ebbing away. She was filled with curiosity about this strange girl and needed to know more.

Betty laughed again, a softer sound this time. "My house was 80 years old when it was destroyed. This house wasn't built until the 1970s."

"How did you die?" Shelley's voice still sounded hoarse.

Betty sighed sadly. "It had been a lovely day - it was me birthday and we had put up the paper chains for Christmas." Seeing Shelley's confused expression, she explained "We never had a Christmas tree like you, but we had these decorations that you made yerself by sticking paper rings together." Shelley nodded, though she still had no idea what a paper chain was.

Betty continued. "I'd just gone up to bed when the air raid siren went off. Me mam ran up the stairs to get me and my little brothers, but then as she bustled us back down, she slipped and twisted her ankle. She was in so much pain, and struggling to walk, but she was only bothered about us getting to the shelter. I pushed and prodded our John and Danny down the garden, got them shut into the shelter, then went back to help me mam. She yelled at me, of course, and tried to get me to leave her, but I was always a stubborn little bugger." She grinned engagingly before her face straightened, as her eyes shone with tears. "Then – boom – the world went black – and that was the end of us both."

Shelley's mouth had dropped open. "How old were you?"

The intensity of Betty's stare increased. "Fifteen – same as you are now, but my life was very different to yours. I'll tell yer what, I'd have died for one of them biccies in your cupboard. We had strict rationing for a while before I was killed. We were often hungry. But we never moaned like you do all the time."

A deep red shame flooded Shelley's face but she couldn't bite back the question she wanted to ask. "Have you been a ghost ever since?" Even to her ears it sounded crass the minute it left her lips.

Betty seemed amused by the question. "Well, I ain't been wandering restlessly shaking me chains the whole time, but yes, I've been around a bit, and I always pop back for the anniversary of when it happened." Her voice quavered a little on her last words, and she dug her heels into the carpet to swing the egg chair fiercely. By the time the chair slowed down, she had recovered herself and carried on a little impatiently. "Describing the whole ghost process would take far too long and that's not why I'm here. Me and me brothers went without lots and were always scared of the bombs, and yet we weren't miserable. But you … you just can't have as many things as you used to and it's like the end of the world. Yer mam works all hours to try to get you things, and you just throw it back in her face. I'm just trying to stop you being an idiot."

For a moment, Shelley was silent. She knew what Betty said was true but didn't know how to answer her. Suddenly a thought struck her. "It's your birthday today, isn't it?"

Betty nodded. "And have I wasted me time being here?"

"No." The girls' eyes met and there were tears in both.

Betty smiled sadly. "Enjoy your life while you..."

The door opened and shut downstairs and a voice said "I'm home." Shelley turned her head towards the door, then turned back to Betty. The chair was empty.

"Betty." She whispered. "Betty, don't go." Shelley felt a sudden desperation to talk more to this funny, brave, bolshy girl who had ceased to be at the age of 15. She wanted to know more about what she was like before the war, what she liked, how she got on with her brothers. She wanted to know if her brothers had survived, stuck in that little shelter. But the chair remained empty, it's gentle swaying gradually stopping.

"Shelley, are you in your room?"

Betty had gone, but the message she had brought with her remained. Pushing herself off the bed, Shelley shouted. "I'm coming, you sit down and I'll get the hot chocolate made ready to decorate the tree."

Jackie

Yuletide Fun Facts

Norwegian scientists have hypothesized that Rudolph's red nose is probably the result of a parasitic infection of his respiratory system.

In Home Alone, the ugly photo of Buzz's girlfriend is actually a boy because director Chris Columbus thought it would be too cruel to make fun of a real girl. The boy used in the picture is the art director's son.

US scientists calculated that Santa would have to visit 822 homes a second to deliver all the world's presents on Christmas Eve, travelling at 650 miles a second.

Many parts of the Christmas tree can actually be eaten, with the needles being a good source of Vitamin C.

There is a village in Peru where people settle the previous year's grudges by fist fighting. They then start the new year off on a clean slate.

The Christmas cracker was invented by a London sweet shop owner called Tom Smith. In 1847, after spotting French bonbons wrapped in paper with a twist at each end, he sold similar sweets with a "love motto" inside. He then included a little trinket and a "bang". His "Bangs of Expectation" included gifts such as jewellery and miniature dolls. By 1900, he was selling 13 million a year.

According to tradition, you should eat one mince pie on each of the 12 days of Christmas to bring good luck - HOWEVER - It's technically illegal to eat mince pies on Christmas Day in England. In the 17th century, Oliver Cromwell banned Christmas pudding, mince pies and anything to do with gluttony. The law has never been rescinded.

Mistletoe is from the Anglo-Saxon word misteltan, which means "little dung twig" because the plant spreads through bird droppings.

The world's largest Christmas stocking was 106 feet 9 inches long and 49 feet 1 inch wide, weighed as much as five reindeer and held almost 1,000 presents. It was made by the Children's Society in London on December 14, 2007.

Mel Tormé's "The Christmas Song" (more commonly known as "Chestnuts Roasting on an Open Fire") was written during a summer heatwave in 1944.

A large part of Sweden's population watches Donald Duck cartoons every Christmas Eve – a tradition that started in 1960.

Jackie

Far

She'd reached a part of the motorway where civilisation had finally conceded to the power of the landscape. Gradually, slip lanes and service stations gave in to looming hills that crept up unannounced behind electricity pylons; casting long, brooding shadows across the chevrons. The cars and lorries encasing her like fractious swarms of wasps five miles ago had long scattered into the last calls of suburbia. Now Sarah drove alone - just her, the car and the setting sun ahead. And her phone, her endlessly ringing phone.

The radio was a pulsing blizzard of hissing conversation and distorted carols as the car swept her under abandoned gantries and bridges. A last flash of music, broken with the fragments of a smashed-up jingle from somewhere further and further away. At last her phone fell silent.

The car carried her westwards with its own will; Sarah's feet rested on the pedals, her chewed down thumbnail bleeding into the steering wheel with every thought. The car followed the dying sun until a metallic shimmer rippled over the skyline: the sea. Road signs returned, confirming that she was still on earth.

"Shame," she muttered into the radio's white noise. A lorry joined her, then another, HGVs with foreign number plates, a couple with little plastic trees with lights twinkling on the dashboards; the drivers' faces pale and tired; the stubble on their chins revealing their own, forgotten miles. The sea devoured the view ahead where a distant ship lit up the grey waves like a floating jewellery box. The car engine moaned with exhaustion. "Not long now," Sarah murmured as they passed the sign for the docks.

"Travelling alone, Miss? Going home for Christmas?" The man at the check-in booth's breath made grey mist with each word. He had very blue eyes set deep within his weather-thrashed face, eyes that had probably seen many like her, those who believed that fresh starts were possible - as long as enough miles were covered first. "Right then, let's have a look..." He frowned at the rain, rain which had changed from delicate wisps to sharpened, ice spears. "Rather you than me!" He took her passport and slid the window shut.

Sarah felt the drum in her chest move upwards as she watched him turn to a faceless colleague behind the glass and ask something. Horizontal rain pierced her arm, dampening the side of the seat. She closed the car window. For a few precious seconds she was safely cocooned inside the fug of the steamy heating with no need to explain herself.

Only a couple of cars queued in front of her; a few lorries to her left. How easy it would be to simply turn around right now and go home again. All the way back *there*. She could just tell the Head she'd had a funny turn that morning: *must have been the remnants of the flu, I'm so sorry...* and had taken the rest of the day off; forgetting to sign out because she'd felt so unwell. Jim wouldn't care; he was too busy with his own job, *God, I've had the shittiest day ever...* He didn't know where she was half the time anyway.

She thought of Annie. Spoilt, bossy, little Annie who loved the childminder more than Sarah - she knew that because Annie told her every night: *Chloe never shouts like you do! I wish you were more like Chloe.* Mind you, it was the childminder she had breakfast and dinner with every day, it was Chloe who Annie told all about her day at nursery. It was her, not Sarah, who'd taken Annie to A&E last week when she'd fallen off the swing - *Chloe's* swing, naturally.

The car in front, an old Renault, was moving slowly towards the ramp. She'd be next. Sarah glanced up at the ferry towering over her, its navy funnels so tall she had to crouch down in her seat to see the top of them. Panic overwhelmed her - was this actually it? Was she really doing this? Finally escaping everything? For the past year, ever since she'd locked herself in the bathroom on New Year's Day, refusing to leave the house; crying tears that were so wild and hysterical they seemed to belong to a stranger, she'd thought of little else. Deep inside her head she could - and did - escape over and over again: flying off to Australia or Africa or even Cornwall, it didn't matter where, as long as she could leave all the noise and demands of that life behind.

Now she here instead, just before Christmas, in a listless line of strangers, about to board the ferry to Ireland. It wasn't planned, despite all the fantasies. Ireland hadn't even been on the list. But she'd driven west instead of east - the motorway diversion had persuaded her - and then she couldn't bring herself to turn back and face another day - and here she was. Her passport and spare phone charger put to use after months of living in her handbag: just in case.

As her heart-rate calmed, she saw the man in the booth's streaky outline motion for her to talk to him again. She reluctantly opened the window as he slid back his pane of glass and communication was resumed.

"Yes, that's all fine, Miss." He returned her passport through thick, fingerless gloves.

"Thanks." She'd passed her credit card over. Her plan was almost official and approved yet now the world had developed a dream-like quality. Like she was starring in a gritty British drama, the backdrop of shut-up warehouses and redundant cranes appropriately grey and bleak.

The man smiled again and glanced upwards. "It's going to be a rough crossing tonight, hope you've got some sea-sick pills?"

He winked at his comment but it was the question mark at the end of his words that bothered her more. She nodded but couldn't return his smile, couldn't let herself get involved with another person, not today. Instead, she glanced behind him. The window hatch was only partially open, probably due to the wind but behind the hi-vis jacket draped over his chair, she glimpsed a portable radiator and a kettle. The urge to abandon this whole stupid idea, cry at him so he'd take pity and let her inside, threatened to overwhelm her. But then she'd have to go back. The moment framed itself importantly in her mind, her conscience a game show host asking,

So, what's it to be, Sarah? It's decision time! Will you, A: Crumple into an emotional mess at this stranger's kind face, have a nice cup of tea then drive home to and face them all or...B: and, take your time now, Sarah, because, remember there's no going back once you're sure...: get a grip of yourself, girl, nod at the man, drive onto the ramp and get yourself on that bloody boat and far away from all this mess?

"Are you all right, Miss?" The man was still there, staring at her, his bushy eyebrows raised.

Sarah heard his concern but took a deep breath before edging the car forward until he was only a fading shape in the mist behind her.

Once onboard, she'd never felt so conspicuous. The ferry was half-empty; no one deliberately choosing to negotiate the Irish Sea in this weather meant the only visible passengers seemed to be construction workers and lorry drivers on a last push for cash before Christmas. They collapsed into chairs in the lounge area once inside, some with tea, others with pints; all waiting for sleep. Nobody talked; the only sound came from the forcefully chirpy announcements. Every time the automatic voice warned them *not to leave their vehicles unlocked or return to them, even in an emergency*, Sarah found herself holding her breath. Her fingers curled stiffly around her phone, switched off in her pocket. They would find her soon. They had to.

Stretched-out minutes passed, each one an agonising reminder that it wasn't too late to go back, she could still say she was taken ill, nobody would know if she changed her mind and went back, they hadn't set sail, not quite, she could just leave the car below deck and disembark, get a coach home. As a distraction, she found a bar in the corner of the lounge and ordered a cup of tea, deliberately avoiding the window. Added a thimbleful of milk, and another, stirring methodically with the plastic stick, carefully opening the sugar sachet and stirring it again, round and round and round. But every swirl seemed to open up a new memory from that morning, like a magic, taunting pool of flashbacks. The fight with Jim. The roundabout where she'd narrowly missed that van.. The bug-eyed stares from class 9b as she'd grabbed her handbag mid-lesson and bolted for the door. The confused questions from the Deputy Head as she'd sprinted past him in reception, her eyes streaming. The hysterical fumbling for her car keys in the staff car park. Battling the traffic, trying to leave town. The bloody diversion. Her phone ringing an hour after she should have come home, after she should have collected Annie from her childminder. Ringing again and again. Ringing, almost in a different, sterner tone just as she passed Birmingham, about the time that Jim would be getting in; throwing his coat over the banister, collapsing like the lorry drivers into a chair before wondering why the hell the house was empty. And the worst one. The one that she'd managed to keep driving away from every time it threatened to catch her up. It was only now, now that she'd been forced to stop that Annie could find her.

"Where are you going?" said Annie accusingly.

Sarah couldn't be sure which had woken her; the lurch of the ferry as it began moving or Annie's voice. She blinked at the little girl in the reindeer jumper who was staring at her knees, which felt damp and hot.

"Why have you spilled tea all over your lap?" asked Annie, except, she realised, it wasn't Annie at all because Annie was over two hundred miles away. The girl stared, waiting for an answer.

"Er, I don't know. I must have fallen asleep or something and..."

"And you didn't put your tea in a safe place first?" asked the girl, clearly enjoying being the grown-up for a change. "That was very dangerous. Tea is very hot, you might've burned yourself, you should be more careful."

Sarah felt her cheeks redden, even though she knew it was ridiculous. But the girl looking accusingly at her was so like Annie, with her large brown eyes and dark blonde hair, as if her own daughter was confronting her, telling her off for running away, wondering why she hadn't come home.

"I'm Aisling," said the girl with the confident tone of someone three times her age. "I'm here with my Daddy. We've been to England to see my Grandma because my Dad's English." She had started to unpeel the Paw Patrol backpack from her shoulders. It looked heavy and took her a couple of goes to swing it up onto the seat next to Sarah's. She chattered away as she unzipped it, tugging so hard at the flimsy canvas Sarah thought it might rip. "My Grandma's nice to me because she feels sorry for me. She lets me have the nice biscuits from the tin, you know, the ones with chocolate on them. She never *says* she feels sorry for me but I know she does. It's because of The Divorce, you see." She paused, noticing the pool of spilt tea glistening on Sarah's side of the table. "I'll just get us something to mop that with." Before Sarah could react, Aisling was at the bar in the corner of the lounge, asking the bemused man for napkins.

Sarah waited obediently, tiredness washing over her, turning her limbs to concrete. She checked the plastic clock on the wall. This time yesterday she'd just finished tucking Annie in after rushing through her bedtime story so she could find enough time to mark another batch of essays. She hadn't made any dinner so they'd had chips from the shop instead on their way back from the childminder. Jim had made himself something, as usual, once he'd driven home from work. She hadn't cared anyway; they still weren't speaking. Her head thumped as she tried to remember why.

She glanced at the bar again, automatically checking for Aisling whom she seemed to have temporarily adopted. Or perhaps it was the other way round - the little girl had such a mature, matronly manner about her, it was hard to tell. Aisling was still there, chattering away to the barman who was now humouring her by flipping beer mats. Sarah's eyes strayed over to the beer pumps in front of them, shiny and welcoming in the bright lounge lights, and then to the fridge just visible behind the bar. Bottles of wine gleamed and winked at her, promising oblivion and sleep. Surely one glass wouldn't hurt? It might help put things into perspective; it usually did, after all. Besides, it wasn't as if Jim was here to tut at her, rolling his eyes as he sanctimoniously sipped an orange juice.

The barman turned to her, barely hiding his relief. "Good evening! What can I get you?" They both looked at Aisling who was still at the bar, providing herself with a running commentary as she tried to perfect her beer mat flipping skills. Sarah smiled at her but Aisling was too engrossed in her task to notice.

"Yours, is she?" asked the barman, or *Connor*, according to the metal badge that was pinned to his shirt.

"A large Chardonnay please, and, God, no, she's not mine, *thank God,* she just started talking to me, that's all," said Sarah, instantly feeling guilty in case Aisling had heard. But she'd gone back to the table where she was happily setting out a colouring book and assorted felt tips.

"Funny little thing, isn't she? I'm not sure who she's with, if she's not with you. I might get someone to check if no-one turns up after a while," said Connor, pouring the amber liquid into a glass.

Sarah shrugged, trying to focus on the girl's welfare rather than the promise of warmth and comfort the wine was already offering. She realised her palms were hurting where her nails were digging into them, trying to stop herself snatching up the whole bottle and running off with it to a solitary corner of the deck where she could drink in peace.

"That's ten Euros, please." Connor acknowledged the flash of panic that crossed her face before adding tactfully, "You can pay by card if it's easier." Gratefully, Sarah found her debit card, checking back at Aisling first. Despite her fierce air of self possession, the little girl looked sad and out of place, colouring determinedly amongst the scattering of snoring truckers. "And a fruit shoot please," she added. Connor obliged with a nod of approval.

"There you are!" said Aisling when Sarah joined her. "Oh, ta, that's very kind of you. I hope you don't mind if I use my teeth for this bit?"

Sarah took a gulp of the wine, relishing the way it instantly loosened her limbs. She shook her head.

With the flourish of an expert, Aisling untwisted the cap with her teeth and bit it off with one clean movement. Sarah took another gulp and smiled at her again.

"Sorry 'bout that," said Aisling before taking a delicate sip, "Grandma always tells me off if I do that. Here," she handed Sarah a blue felt tip, "You have this one so you can help me do the sky."

Dutifully, Sarah obeyed and the two of them coloured in the picture of the Disney castle with its turrets and flags in a comfortable silence. The boat's engines throbbed steadily somewhere deep below their feet and the lounge gently tipped and shuddered in unison. Relieved at the change of pace and Aisling's quieter mood, Sarah allowed her mind to wander.

That morning, Jim had finally said it. Muttered the words like a whispered full stop, not designed for her to hear but she had. He'd turned away from her, his shoulders tight, threw his plate into the sink but the clatter hadn't managed to mask it -

"Control freak."

Sarah had swallowed the words down like a bitter cough sweet, sucked and chewed them as she'd left the house, exhaling them back as a poisoned cloud into the icy, mid December air. "Of course I'm a bloody control freak, Jim," she'd whispered at the de-icer. "What else is there room for me to be?"

"Don't be indulgent, Sarah," she instructed herself, recalling some self-help blog she'd read recently, one of many. She sprayed furious chemical scribbles onto the windscreen, "Stop it. Get over it; you'll feel better soon. Move on. Stop over-reacting." She placed the can back carefully in its allocated space in the boot, next to her over-sized bag neatly packed with schemes of work and marked books and got into the driving seat. Turned the key in the ignition and waited. Checked her watch to see if she'd be late. She dreaded being late. Panic swept through her in a single, violent wave. Teenagers couldn't wait. Especially not her class.

It had been colder inside the car than out that morning. It felt so long ago now it may as well have been another time all together. She often wished she *did* live in another time. Perhaps a time when people worked because they wanted to, only spent money when they needed to and not out of some terrible compulsion to make everything better. Perhaps a time when people only drank for pleasure, not necessity. She'd revved the engine, which sounded as anxious and petulant as she felt, and waited for Jim to appear in the driveway with an apologetic smile on his face.

He didn't come. The only apologetic smile she glimpsed that morning was Annie's as her tear-stained face peered down at her from the bedroom window.

"Don't let her see you cry, Sarah," she'd told the dashboard as she pulled out into the road. The numbers on the car clock had glowed in a neon warning against the dim morning light. It was already 7:43am. That gave her exactly 21 minutes to battle through the traffic, providing she didn't lose two minutes at the lights.

"Maybe I am a control freak, Jim," she continued, braking furiously at the roundabout, "but if you'd had my upbringing, *Mr Perfectly-Spoiled-Home-Counties,* maybe you'd understand why I react the way I do!" She released the handbrake and accelerated onto the roundabout, squealing to a halt as she narrowly missed a car. Someone behind her, some idiot in an orange van, had honked their horn. Something about the sound of it - such a self-important noise - led her to uncoil the tight, ingrained ball of fury she'd been nurturing inside for months.

And that was when she'd snapped.

Before she knew what she was doing, Sarah found herself banging on the van driver's window, her own car abandoned in front, its door wide open, steaming fumes into the screaming, passing traffic.

"Oi!" yelled a voice that sounded exactly like her own, except it couldn't be, because her voice was calm and measured and, well, always in control.

The driver, dumbstruck, stared at her through the frosty glass.

"What the *fuck* do you think you're doing?" the furious imposter inside Sarah ranted.

"Hey! Come on!" yelled someone behind them in the queue that had been building impatiently, "Some of us have got jobs to go to!"

"So have I!" screamed Sarah, pausing in shock at herself, so horribly out of control, so unrecognisable, "So have I! So have I!" To her disbelief, tears from nowhere were streaming down her scarlet cheeks, tears she had no idea how to control.

The van driver had looked the other way.

"I got these for you both." Connor's voice shocked Sarah back to the present. "Hope you don't mind, you both looked so busy there, I thought you might like some more refreshment." He placed another fruit shoot and glass of wine on the table. He glanced at Sarah and smiled at Aisling. He looked red-eyed and pale; the look of someone well into a double shift. Carefully laying his tray on the adjacent table, he crouched down until he was level with Aisling's busy, stooped head. "What's that you're doing? Aisling, wasn't it?" His voice was soft, he seemed to be used to children but Sarah detected a hint of anxiety behind it.

Aisling stopped abruptly and stared at him. "I would have thought that was obvious." she said, not bothering to hide her scorn. "I'm *colouring*! Can't you see that?"

Connor blushed faintly, he couldn't have been more than twenty, realised Sarah as she took another sip of wine. She blushed herself. What on earth must she look like to him? A woman nearing forty with bad roots and sweaty work clothes, steadily getting drunk on Chardonnay on a ferry, accompanied only by someone else's child. A child she didn't even know. He'd probably alerted the ports without her knowing - *suspicious looking woman onboard: possible child abduction.*

But Connor's attention was firmly on Aisling. "Oh yes, so you are. Sorry, Aisling. I was just wondering, as you're not actually *with* this nice lady..."

Aisling sighed at him and put down the purple pen she'd been brandishing. "What do you mean, not with her? I am *with* her! I'm right here sat next to her!"

Connor's cheeks coloured again. If she hadn't been so worried about his real intentions, Sarah might have felt sorry for him. She took another sip, Aisling clearly took no prisoners.

"No, no, what I mean is, who did you come onto the ferry with, Aisling? Where are your parents?"

That was the wrong thing to ask. Aisling's face immediately clouded over like the night outside as she shrugged at him, before returning to the castle which was now an angry shade of purple.

Sarah took another swig of wine, before nudging her gently. "We're only wondering, Aisling," she said, "We just want to check that you're ok." Sarah searched her wine-fogged brain, trying to remember their earlier conversation. "Didn't you mention your Dad? Didn't you say you'd just been visiting your Grandma, in England? Was it an early Christmas visit?"

As Aisling looked up, Sarah was surprised to see a couple of tears trying to hide behind her dark lashes.

"My Dad's here somewhere, "she whispered. "But since we left Grandma's house he's been really cross. I think it's because my Mummy's coming to meet me when we get back to Ireland

and he always gets angry when he thinks about her."

She took a deep breath. Sarah could see how hard she was trying to be brave. She looked so much like Annie: her poor, poor, little Annie who'd had to hold back her own tears so much lately.

Aisling sniffed and fixed her dark eyes on Sarah. "It's because my Mummy's been very stressed lately," she said seriously, *too seriously for someone so young*, thought Sarah. "Daddy says it's because she's working too much, and worrying about everything and because," she paused and looked at Sarah's empty glass, "...and because of all the wine she drinks. And because of The Divorce."

Sarah got up unsteadily, lurching with the rhythm of the boat. "Sorry. I need some fresh air. Connor, would you watch Aisling?"she asked before going outside to the deck.

The sudden change in temperature hit her like an icy wall. The wind screeched in her ears, freezing her neck as she wrestled the heavy door shut, taking a few seconds to find her balance. She cursed her flimsy work jacket and heels; as cold and thin as wet paper. Regrets flew up and spat at her in the punishing sea-spray. *What have you done? How could you leave Annie behind like that? What about Jim? He's not so bad, is he? And what about work? This is ridiculous Sarah! What the hell are you going to do when you get to bloody Ireland, anyway? What about money? Where will you stay? Stupid girl! Stupid, stupid, Sarah! That's what you get for trying to be spontaneous!*

Pale lights swung from the railings but the sky remained black and solid, the water hurled up from the waves merging into biting sheets of rain. The deck was empty. Only the occasional soaking gull brave enough to face the elements soared overhead. She forced herself across a few sodden feet of decking to reach the side of the boat, slick with water as she leaned against it, peering nervously down at the threatening waves beneath. She pictured them all as if from above, an illustration in Annie's atlas at home, a handful of confused strangers trapped together on a tiny toy ship, stranded in the blue between the craggy edges of land. Stuck in the middle of the page, trying to leave and trying to return, all at the same time. What a mess.

"Got a light?" The man who'd suddenly appeared next to her was English too, judging by his accent. He was far more drunk than she was, lurching even more than the bows of the juddering boat. She glanced at him, blinking furiously against the driving rain. He was a little younger than her, unshaven, with just a thin jumper and jeans, *ridiculous out here*, she thought, before remembering her own, flimsy clothes.

She shook her head at him and he sighed. "No worries, sorry to bother you."

As he turned away, Sarah caught his dark, familiar eyes, red rimmed, a couple of tears trying to hide inside the lashes. He said something else to her, she thought, but the wind threw his words away, sent them flying off into the sky and down into the blackness.

Was that Aisling's father? She'd heard the same sorrow in his voice, it lingered in the frozen air, the catch in his throat, its broken gasp. She recognised the desperation of another broken person because she was one herself. For a brief moment the roar of the storm and its thunderous waves seemed to eclipse everything else.

"Wait!" she called after him but he'd gone. The only reply was the sound of the storm laughing in her face. She had to find Aisling.

Stooping low beneath the railings, Sarah wrapped her saturated arms around herself and slowly, deliberately, aimed her feet back to the safety of the lounge, the wind fighting her every step. A loud sob forced her to turn back. Aisling's father was crouched on top of the railings, his tears mixing with the unforgiving sea-spray whipping up from the mouth of the waves beneath him.

Clarity hit her hard. Aisling didn't deserve this. She hadn't asked for any of it- she was more than a bi-product of all these adult problems.

Her father couldn't drown, no matter how desperate he was. It wasn't fair. She wouldn't allow it.

"No! Don't!" she screamed. She lunged forward, tried to grab him but the storm knocked her back. His empty, pleading eyes, Aisling's eyes, met hers for a long second - a second of eerie silence as the tempest took its next breath - that was all it took to hear the awful splash. A neat, rounded sound in contrast to the chaos of the storm; clear and distinct.

And then suddenly everyone was there, circled round Sarah as she stood, shivering and dripping in front of the bar, Connor and little Aisling watching with their mouths open; the truckers who'd woken up and were leaning in to listen to her, horror etched over their sleepy faces. Someone put a warm blanket over her as the tannoy burst into life and there was an alarm ringing somewhere from the deck outside and people, staff, running in different directions, slamming doors; the beating wings of a helicopter somewhere. Connor gave her a whisky to calm her frantic mind. A woman, a kind woman in a uniform, talked to her for a while, asked her questions about the man on the deck. And through all of it, Sarah held sobbing Aisling tight, Aisling whose eyes were as dark and wide as the depths of the sea. Aisling who had screamed and yelled for Sarah when anyone had tried to part them. Curled up together behind the table still scattered with felt-tips, Sarah shivered and thought of Annie, and Jim.

They slept until the sun came up and the coast of Ireland beckoned. Sarah and this little, lost girl who'd adopted her so fiercely.

"Sarah? Sarah, is that you? Oh my God, I'm so glad, I can't believe you just...left like that! Are you okay, Sarah? We've been so worried about you! I read about that man, jumping, it's terrible, isn't it? How's the little girl, she's back with her mum, isn't she? Thank God. Oh, right, yes, hang on...I love you, Sarah, you do know that, don't you? Yep, *hang on, Annie*, look, Sarah, we can sort it out, work, money, all of it, we'll see how we can make things work without you feeling...well, like that again. I love you, please come home, Sarah...*yes, okay, Annie!*"

A scuffling sound, a pause.

"Mummy? Where are you? I've missed you! Are you enjoying your holiday? When are you coming home? I want to show you my bedroom; Daddy helped me tidy it all up for you. And I've done you a Santa picture! Are you coming home?"

Sarah managed to speak, though it was difficult. She didn't want Annie to hear her cry. She had to be brave.

"Yes, Annie. I love you very much. And yes, I'm coming home."

Sally

Boxing Day Walk

I had my friends over for Christmas in Cork
And bravely suggested a Boxing Day walk.
They all thought I was pretty barmy,
Apart from Dev, my mate from the army.
He said "That sounds pretty cool,
Five miles round the local pool.
Eventually they all agreed.
So Dev and I, we took the lead.
We set off at a steady pace.
Till Debbie said "This ain't a race."
"Ooh look." I said, "At those birds soaring".
And someone whispered "God, she's boring!"
I knew morale was getting lower
As everyone got slower and slower.
Sadie wailed "How much more?"
"My feet are getting really sore."
"I told you those trainers were way too new."
Said Clive, adding grimly. "I need the loo."
We got home while it was still light.
Although we looked a sorry sight.
Johnny had started to sneeze and cough.
And Sadie had taken her shoes and socks off.
Kerry had tripped and grazed her knee,

And Clive was desperate for a wee.
Next year, I'll forget the walk, I think.
I'll take my friends out for a drink

Jackie

Olivia

Olivia pulled at the top drawer, and pulled again. The dressing table refused to comply - its wood was stiff and Victorian and didn't take kindly to such rough treatment.

"For God's sake, *open*!" Olivia muttered, before pressing her lips into a thin line of determination. She applied both her hands this time; taking care not to smudge her freshly varnished nails, and gave it one more heave. In an act of defiance, the dressing table released the drawer below instead - which crashed open, covering the cream carpet with blusher and shadow in shades of plum and taupe, peach and copper. Rubbing at the powder with a facecloth only blended it in further so Olivia tried rosewater, dabbing at the stains with a scented tissue until the floor resembled a fluffy oil painting.

A glimpse of the purple, velvet box – an old but precious Christmas gift - in front of the mirror propelled her into action. Six o'clock already and she hadn't even opened the wine! What would David think if he could see her like this? Abandoning the colourful mess in the bedroom, she swept downstairs in a flurry of pink silk, her wet hair trailing in mahogany coils, and scanned the drinks cabinet for the crystal glass.

And now for some carols from Kings' murmured the radio and she smiled as she sipped. By the time the radio spoke again Olivia was on her second glass. As was the custom every Christmas Eve, she carried the remainder of the bottle carefully upstairs to begin her work.

With trembling fingers, Olivia unwrapped the first of several containers-in-waiting to the purple, velvet box which waited, centre stage. She took her time; releasing the lotion from its smooth, claret-coloured packaging; massaging its expensive scent into her skin: the smell of Christmas.

Carefully replacing it, she picked up the second; the heavy bottle satisfyingly cold in her hand. This cream was the most expensive but the girl behind the counter had assured her that "true class don't come cheap" and Olivia knew David was a man of taste. She slowly massaged the lotion into her body, eyes closed, enjoying the sensation of silk. The wine had seduced her and as she relaxed into the moment, she thought again of David.

And now for a special performance of Silent night... lulled the radio somewhere below the stairs but Olivia was lost in her ritual and could no longer hear. Methodically, she worked her way along the line of cleansers, toners, moisturisers and once her skin no longer felt like her own she added a complicated blend of foundations and powders to the canvas. More wine was poured, the top drawer slid effortlessly open and the painting finally began. The purple velvet box watched approvingly as a web of colour spread across her face; illuminating her features with shadow and light, mascara and sparkle. Blood-scarlet finished her lips and the ceremony closed with a dress of soft, white satin; diamonds and shoes as elegant as the city skyline. The door banged shut as she tripped into the night, finally ready for David.

***

As she reached the bus shelter at exactly half past nine, the doorman recognised her immediately. He watched her settle herself on the wet, plastic seats, gazing across the road at the fairy-lit hotel. Like she did every sodding year. The puddles seemed to cast her in a personal spotlight; the moon exposing her plastic jewels and cheap shoes.

She looked so frail and frozen, the doorman shivered. He watched her soaking nightgown ripple, the wind cut through the thin material like an icy blade; they said it'd be a white Christmas this year, mind you that's what they said every bloody year. He fumbled around in his pocket, trying to find his mobile, scrolling down the list until he found the number for local social services - the same ones who helped out with his mum. There must be someone: social services, the police, the home up the road; surely *someone* could take her away and look after her, especially tonight. Why wasn't she an old folks' home, looking forward to a nice Christmas dinner tomorrow? Some relatives visiting to pull a cracker, share a joke and a sherry or whatever they did in those places? Shame on him; he should have made the call last Christmas Eve, or the one before that, or the one before that...

But as he began to tap out the number, something stopped him, just as it always did. Her smile. The old lady looked so happy, so *contented* as she sat there in the rain, mascara leaking down into her wrinkles.

A sudden rattle from the hotel doors spurred him into action and he opened them graciously for one of the restaurant's regulars, Sir David Bellingham.

"Good Night, Sir, Merry Christmas," The doorman held his umbrella over the elderly man, sprightly and dapper in his Saville Row suit.

"Ah yes, of course, the same to you. Damn! Look, sorry to bother you, old chap but I seem to have mislaid something again, it must be my age. I don't suppose you'd be so kind as to..."

As the doorman helped him hunt in vain for something dropped on the pavement, he thought no more about the old lady in the bus shelter. He didn't notice her cross the road whilst his back was turned, darting down to retrieve something shiny from the shadows close by. Moments later, with Sir David safely inside a black cab, he realised she'd vanished into the night.

***

Back at the dressing table, Olivia presented the purple velvet box with its reward. She fingered the pure gold cuff link longingly and thought again of her David before adding it to the rest of her collection. She studied the silver lighter, the dropped receipts, the comb and her prize exhibit: his door key. This was his best Christmas present so far. At last, the chance to finally meet him.

She closed the box.

Sally

The Magpie Secret

"Don't look!" Carol jokingly covered her sister's eyes with the palm of her hand. They were enjoying their weekly meet up in the little café in the park. In Summer, it was hard to get a seat here, but today they had their pick of tables. Marny thought it was a shame; admittedly wet Autumn days didn't really tempt her out, but on crisp frosty December mornings like this, nothing was nicer than a walk through the park followed by hot chocolate and cake in this quirky little café.

Gently pushing Carol's hand away, Marny saw the magpie sat on the windowsill studying her, his head on one side. Her eyes scoured the area. "Oh no, he's on his own, isn't he?" Her tone was light, but they both knew she took single magpie sightings very seriously. They had history with her.

"Fraid so." Carol laughed and changed the subject. "That waitress behind the counter, I haven't seen her before, but she seemed to know you. Was she here when you worked here?"

Marny frowned. "No, she was a customer at the time. But I only did three shifts, remember?" Marny had taken on a few shifts a couple of years before to supplement her income, but on her third shift had fallen over the hoover while cleaning up, torn ligaments in her foot and ended up on crutches for weeks. She'd had to take sick leave from her main job and ended up in debt. She had always blamed the magpie she had shooed away from an outdoor table just moments before it happened.

***

"Something's bothering you, isn't it?" Carol asked as they wandered back through the park. "If it's about the house, then don't fret. Leave everything until after Christmas and we can sort it out and put it up for sale in the new year. Greg and I don't need the money urgently"

Marny scowled as another magpie hopped across in front of her, and wondered if it could credibly be linked to the one at the café to make a pair. She knew that, unlike her, Carol was comfortably off, but she also knew that her and Greg had dreams they would like to follow – and they certainly deserved to enjoy their dreams after all they'd been through recently. They'd never had children and had always aspired to travel the world. But Carol was right, there was something bothering her. It sat in the way of the sale of the house and its name was Frank. Carol had never known the truth about Frank, only that he was the father who lived with her for a few years and who she never saw again after he left. She was the younger sister and much had been kept from her.

Misinterpreting the reason for Marny's silence, Carol said "It doesn't need to be that soon. Springtime will do. And Greg and I will come round and help you with the sorting out and the DIY stuff." She touched Marny's arm. Turning to look into her sister's pale face,

Marny's eyes were drawn to the strands of thin, new hair, poking out underneath Carol's thick woolly hat. Her heart contracted painfully.

"No, it's fine. I'm well onto the sorting out. A lot has gone to the charity shop – you know what a hoarder mum was – but anything that might be special, I'll save for you to have a look through. Leo is coming home for Christmas, so he can earn his keep and do some jobs around the house."

Carol smiled brightly at the mention of her only nephew. "How is Leo? Is he buckling down to Uni yet or is he still being a little sod?"

Marny raised her eyebrows. "The latter. But a lovable little sod all the same."

Carol laughed and glanced upwards to a magpie sat alone in a sycamore tree. "So, remind me, how many other times have lonely magpies caused you grief?"

"Oh, let me count. The day before I lost my job, a couple of days before I broke up with John, a week before I got scammed..."

"You can't blame magpies for everything."

"I can."

***

When they parted, Marny walked the short distance to the house she had grown up in. Carol was so grateful for her moving back in and sorting out their mother's house when she died, but in reality, withstanding the awful circumstances, it had been the answer to her prayers. She had been juggling bills and income for years, but she had reached the position where her only choices would have been to re-mortgage or sell her house and downsize. Moving into her mother's huge old house had allowed her to quickly sell her own house and store all the possessions she decided to keep in rooms she had already cleared. She was using her spare time to deep clean and decorate the house and had the peace of mind of knowing that when the house was sold, her half of the proceeds would easily buy a small house in a nice area near to her sister. The money from the sale of her own house provided something she'd never had before – savings! Or that was the plan before Frank reared his ugly head.

She made a decision before reaching home and the minute the door closed behind her, she rang the number Frank had given her in the message he had sent her out of the blue.

"Hello." The voice was weak, sounded unsure of itself and Marny wondered if she had the right number.

"Frank?"

"Who's this?" he asked suspiciously.

"Marny."

"Oh." A pause. "You got my message then?"

"Yes, I got your message." Her voice was hard. "And you don't deserve a penny out of my mother's house. You bled her dry while you lived with her."

"Doesn't matter what you think, it's whether I'm legally entitled, isn't it?" His voice was raised yet still sounded thin. But there was no mistaking the arrogance and aggression in his voice. Same old Frank.

She doubted Frank would have a chance in hell in the courts. He'd moved into her mother's house a few years after her father had died and had rarely contributed to anything. The only good thing that had come from her mother's relationship with Frank had been Carol and he had walked out of her life when she was five years old, never paying a penny towards supporting her. Marny was determined to prevent him getting anything from them now.

"You want to chance your arm and the court costs of trying to take money from us, do you, Frank?"

She heard the sneer. "Won't cost me anything. I'll get legal aid. I've not worked for years, so you'll be denying a sick man his rightful money, that's how it will look in court."

Marny sucked in her breath. Calling his bluff wasn't going to be easy, so reluctantly she offered to meet him. Thinking he had the upper hand, he pushed her to arrange it somewhere of his choice. He could no longer drive, would need to come on the train, and wanted to do it the following week. It all suited Marny well - she didn't want to meet him too close to home and wanted it over and done with as soon as possible, and so she swallowed her desire to appear in charge for now. She arranged to meet him in a café just down the road from Barturnton station, a bleak little unmanned outpost of a station, 11 miles away from her home, the following Tuesday.

***

She arrived early, parked in a nearby car park and walked to the café. She ordered an oat milk latte. "It'll look a bit lonely without one of our lovely cakes." The waiter was around Leo's age, with blonde floppy hair and a wide grin. His badge told her his name was Joe.

She smiled at him. "They do look lovely, but I don't think I could keep one down today. Next time, though."

The smile left his face, and he frowned in concern. "Are you okay?"

She nodded. "Yeah, just a meeting I'm not looking forward to, that's all."

She chose a table at the far end of the café, which was a reasonable distance from any of the other tables, but still in clear sight of the rest of the room. It was important that she took charge of this conversation from the very beginning and she had dressed carefully for the meeting. She took a few deep breaths, crossed her legs and sat back to wait for him.

He was late; from her viewpoint she saw him arrive and search the room anxiously before heading over towards her. She noticed the limp straight away, and wondered cynically if he was putting it on. But the sallow skin, the dark rings under his eyes and the thinness told another story. This was a man who was ill alright, but his expression was still antagonistic and he dispensed with any greeting as he scraped the chair back and dropped down onto it to stare her in the face. "Well?"

Marny met his stare and crossed her arms over her chest. "I'm here to find out exactly what you want."

He sniffed and removed the black woollen cap he was wearing to reveal a mass of stringy grey hair, which looked as though it hadn't been washed in weeks. He slung the cap down on the chair next to him. Marny saw that his hands were trembling. "£20,000," he said suddenly.

The words stunned her. She started to laugh, enjoying the release of a tension she hadn't even realised she'd been holding in, before anger snapped her out of it and leaning quickly forward, she hissed at him. "You're nuts, if you think you're going to get anything like that off me."

He was clearly rattled and swallowed twice before muttering defensively. "Well, maybe we should ask Carol what she thinks."

Marny was still leaning forward in his face, and her voice became menacing. "This is between you and I. IF I decide to give you a single penny, and it is a big if, it will be from my money, not from the house sale. And I will have papers drawn up by a solicitor, which you will sign forfeiting your right to any claim on the house and agreeing not to contact either of us, or any member of our family again."

"Now why would you want to do that?" His eyes narrowed. "Carol doesn't know you're here, does she?"

Out of the corner of her eye, she noticed Joe pass by close to their table. She shifted her weight back slightly and lifted the cup to her lips, playing for time as much as anything. When she spoke, her voice was clear and calm, unlike her insides. "I will give you £5000 if you agree to the terms now. Otherwise, you get nothing."

Frank seemed to struggle with this. He stared down at his shaking hands and shook his head. Marny could hear his chest wheezing and when he finally looked up and spoke, his breath was ragged. "All right, I'll take it. But you'd better get it me quick." He began to cough and Marny did the decent thing and fetched him a glass of tap water from the dispenser at the end of the service counter.

He gulped down the water and looked across the table, his demeanour calmer now. "How is Carol?" he asked.

How was Carol? Carol, who had gone through hell this year, lost her breast through cancer and her hair through chemo? Part of her wanted to scream at this loathsome man just how much his daughter had suffered. But it was not his business and she wasn't going to share any part of Carol or herself with him.

"If you wanted to know how your daughter was, you should have contacted her years ago – or maybe paid a penny towards supporting her."

"If she ever was my daughter." Frank's eyes met Marny's and they were watery. "Your mother had someone else on the side while I lived with her. She thought I didn't know." His mouth twisted nastily. "Maybe that's why she never went after me for maintenance?"

Marny felt bile rise in her throat. She hated Frank for many reasons, but meeting his eyes still, she knew he was goading her through bitterness and for reasons she couldn't pin down in her mind, it rang true. And who could blame her mother, knowing how Frank had treated her – how he'd treated them all. Her head pounded with anger and frustration as she thought of how hard she had worked all her life, how much she had endured and overcome, and now this awful man who she thought she'd seen the last of years ago was enjoy taunting her while he took her money off her.

Her distress was palpable and he was enjoying this now. "Maybe Carol should go looking for her other possible daddy." He smiled spitefully. "He might be more to your liking than me."

Something snapped and she grabbed his glass of water and threw it in his face. She heard the murmurs of shock from the closest tables to them, but she had lost all control and shouted wildly at him. "Any scrap of humanity would be better than you. You're a nasty arrogant bully who controlled the whole family with your fists and your temper. I hope you really are ill and you never get to spend a penny of the money you've blackmailed me for. The world will be better off when you're dead and I'm damned sure no-one will ever miss you!"

The gasps of shock and murmurs of disapproval had grown all around her throughout her tirade. At a nearby table, a child burst into tears, and she was aware of Joe crossing the café towards her.

Frank tried to jump to his feet and stumbled, grabbing the table to prevent falling. For the first time, she became aware of the stale odour that surrounded him, and the stains on his worn and ripped sweatshirt. Her temper spent, she covered her face with her hands, desperate to hide the tears welling up inside her.

"I think you should leave." She recognised the voice and lifted her face to apologise shame-facedly to Joe. But he was addressing Frank who backed off without a word and limped across to the door. "Do you want another coffee – on the house? You look as though you need one." Joe smiled down kindly at her.

She smiled back. "No, but thank you. I'll take a few minutes then go home."

As she stood to leave, she noticed the cap left on the chair. It looked greasy and a couple of wiry grey hairs clung to it. It repulsed her in the same way its owner did but as she turned to leave, an idea came to her and she grabbed the dirty cap and threw it in her bag.

***

Carol rang the following evening for their usual Wednesday night chat. She was disgruntled as she had missed a promised meal out the night before due to Greg's train being delayed.

"Would you believe it, someone jumped off the bridge at Barturnton. Of all places! It's not even a proper station there. Does anyone even get on and off there these days?"

A sick feeling came over Marny. "What time was this? Do they know who it was?"

"About 4 o'clock apparently and they said it was a man in his 70s. I'm surprised you haven't seen it on social media. Rumour has it he was homeless as he was so unkempt."

Any other time, Marny would have laughed at her sister's characteristic penchant for gossip even around the darkest of topics, but the certainty in her mind that this was Frank filled her with guilt and horror. Frank was a vile man, but he was undoubtedly sick and still possibly Carol's father, and the idea that her harsh words might have driven him to take his own life appalled her.

Carol had moved on. "The Park Café are starting their Christmas lunches at the weekend. Do you fancy going a bit later on Saturday and having a festive buttie?"

***

The café was busy, but Carol had booked a window table overlooking the duck pond, and they sat contentedly watching children playing while they caught up on each other's news from the week – well, most of it in Marny's case.

Marny had agonised long and hard since the meeting with Frank, and especially since the news of his death – and she was certain beyond doubt that it was him. She had considered telling Carol the whole story, but couldn't bear the thought of the distress it might cause her. She had toyed with the idea of secretly getting DNA tested from Frank's cap. It would be easy to get DNA from Carol who shed hair all the time in her company. And if Frank turned out not to be Carol's father, then maybe a sisterly Christmas gift of a subscription with a DNA matching company could find out who was. The problem was that on the one hand Marny felt that Carol deserved the chance to find her father if he was still out there, and on the other, she had enjoyed her life this far without a father figure, so why risk disappointing and possibly hurting her? She had still not made a decision.

"Do you think Leo will want to come to ours with you for Christmas Day?" Carol looked expectantly at Marny. Since she had been on her own, Carol had ensured that Marny and Leo never spent a Christmas alone.

"Yes, I'm sure he will. Oh wow, look at all those magpies." They both silently counted the magpies.

"Seven. What does that mean, Marny?"

"Seven for a secret never to be told." Marny answered slowly. The magpies had just given her the answer to her dilemma. Carol had all the family she needed.

Jackie

Feline Sleepy

Colin always left it at least ten minutes before he gave the signal. Sometimes the human came back after locking up. The human was quite forgetful, like much of his species - often having to re-raise the shop shutters and deactivate the alarm before climbing inside his noisy metal box and disappearing into the night. Sometimes he'd leave his jacket draped over the office chair.

That night it seemed he was never going to leave at all. Perhaps it was something to do with the bottles and chocolates he'd consumed earlier with the other humans. They'd been miserable at first but the more of the bubbly liquid they consumed and the more they sang and danced, they happier they became. Some of them had silly crowns made of paper perched on their heads; others pulled colourful tubes that exploded and made Colin jump, even though he was watching from the outside. The left-over human faffed with the alarm for ages in the drizzle, re-entered the shop to retrieve his phone and then remembered he'd forgotten to cash-up.

Perched in a queue on the fire escape steps, Colin and the other cats grew impatient. Rain and mist had spiked their fur and icy droplets hung from their whiskers. Collected cat-breath formed tiny fog clouds. Several yawned, but that was nothing unusual.

When the human finally departed, Colin gave his customary yowl.

BOOM! Twenty determined cat heads hit the back door in solid unison, it gave way like paper, naturally the human hadn't locked it. Colin padded through behind them, relishing the chaos as they charged towards the shop floor. The rows of beds, many accompanied by lamps and *Sale!* banners beckoned enticingly under the security lights. A loud, unified purr thrummed through the air as each cat debated: king size? Cabin? Futon? Standard queen?

As the OAP cats headed unsteadily towards the orthopaedic mattress section and the kittens raced to the bunk beds, Colin hissed at a rival tom hurtling his way. After a brief fight on his favourite double, Colin won and settled down for a casual wash.

With every bed in the store now occupied, each cat drifted peacefully off to sleep.

Sally

Christmas Film and TV Quiz

1. Which Doctor made his debut in the show's 2005 festive special called The Christmas Invasion?

2. In The Vicar of Dibley's 1996 Christmas special, which actor guest starred as Tristan Campbell, who ended up proposing to Geraldine on Christmas Day?

3. Which classic comedy's Christmas special ended with Tim and Dawn finally finding love?

4. How old is Kevin McCallister in Home Alone?

5. According to 1946's Christmas classic It's Wonderful Life, what happens every time a bell rings?

6. Which comic actress appeared in the TARDIS wearing a wedding dress in a Doctor Who Christmas special?

7. In Will Ferrell's Elf, what's the first rule in the Code of The Elves?

8. What is the name of the British boy band Billy Mack is competing against for Christmas Number One in Love Actually?

9. What feel-good song is everyone dancing to in the final scene of The Holiday?

10. Die Hard takes place on Christmas Eve -
    but in which city?

Jackie

Jayden's Christmas Journey

My name's Jayden. My mum's choice – my dad said no-one would know if I was a girl or a boy with that name – and to be fair, a few people have been a bit confused – but I'm a girl! And mum was always going to get her own way. "She wears the trousers" dad says. I think I'm going to be quite like my mum when I'm older. I've had my moments of getting a bit feisty – just ask mum!

I'd been sleepy for a while, though and I think mum was getting a bit worried about me. Then when I woke up, I felt a whooshing feeling around my head. I had an urge I'd never felt before. I had to get out, I needed air, but I didn't know why.

Everything felt different. I twisted and turned but was trapped and I felt a throbbing sensation all around me. My heart was racing, I got distressed and I knew that mum was upset too. It seemed to go on forever.

And then, suddenly I felt free but bright lights blinded me. I was terrified, but mum was happy. Dad had his arm around her shoulder and looked really happy too. I couldn't see very much but it was a strange world, very different to what I'd been used to. There was noise and laughter and someone in a gown and mask shouted "Congratulations! Our first Christmas baby this year. What are you calling her?"

"Jayden!" they both shouted.

Jackie

The Computer Garden

The planes never did fall out of the sky. Below the metal death machines the people threw themselves into the celebrations, rolling and cavorting across pub carpets or ploughing through tins of Quality Street, but one eye always remained on the clouds. Perhaps this was when it was all to come full circle. Perhaps technology had finally started to eat itself and those who created it. Soon the fateful digits 00 would click into place and civilisation held its breath.

Charlie Stafford wanted to hold his breath too but his asthma prevented it. The glittering predators overhead hovered level with distant tower blocks in the distance. The waking hum of his new computer combined with the dull drone of one the last incoming planes of the century. It was peaceful, until fireworks shattered through his thoughts.

Next Tuesday, then, called his wife from the bottom of the stairs, although it may as well

128

have been Jupiter, so far away was she from him, *Make sure you're not in.*

She didn't slam the front door. It might have been more dramatic, perhaps more sincere, if she had. Only a faint jingle followed by a thud as her keys fell through the letter box marked the occasion. No point waiting for the rings to follow. They never did get round to all that. He chewed his thumb-nail; *so the bitch had finally gone.* He gnawed at the nail again and again until he tore the quick. The searing sting helped a bit but it wasn't enough. The blood tasted ok though. The metal soothed him.

Bloody fireworks. He resumed his spy-hole at the bay, protected on the third floor, the shabby Victorian semi was a blockade against society. Another firework; a cheer in the distance. The city was a glittering jewellery box tonight, reflected by the skating satellites and lurking planes. *She was down there somewhere, speeding through the sodden streets.* Charlie pulled so hard on the velvet a curtain ring splintered somewhere above his left ear. His heart banged briefly in his chest, it made him cough. He checked the time, yanked the curtains shut and commenced his computer game.

Minutes crept by, then hours. The new century arrived somewhere below the living room window, there were more fireworks and nothing that was supposed to fell out of the sky. Charlie barely noticed. He had enemies to fire at and dangerous lands to conquer. The virtual world offered far more to Charlie than the 21st century ever could, he knew that without even sampling it first.

Slowly, gradually, the hours melted into days, then weeks. When he was hungry he ordered food from the internet, they delivered it up the fire escape outside his bedroom. When he wanted to communicate, he entered chat rooms, when he wanted sex he watched pornography and when his eyes burned he passed out in his chair. As watery, wintery sunshine tried to break through his curtained fortress, his spine developed a pronounced curve. Arthritis invaded his finger joints but he knew he had to kill the enemies who faced him constantly on the screen; he had to choose his weapons with precision and care; he had to look after his comrades, despite his physical hardships.

Bloody 'ell, mate, said the man from the computer warehouse when he delivered the next model, puffing and panting as he dragged the new machine up the fire escape, *How long since you had a wash?*

Charlie didn't hear, his new machine glinted splendidly as it beeped into life. With a sneer of disgust he heaved his old companion across to the window, pulled up the blinds for the first time in months and threw it, screaming, into the garden beneath. The computer warehouse man gazed at him wide-eyed, he knew Charlie's type. *Careful, Mate,* he said, *you might get done for that.* But Charlie couldn't hear.

The new machine was faster, more stream-lined than the first but Charlie didn't trust her. He tried to ignore her beauty and concentrated on his armies, the invasions, his men needed him more. But still she taunted him with the brightness of her screen and comforting touch of her mouse. *Slut.*

Time passed and still she mocked him. The moonlight joined her, making him weary and irrational. One night his rage exploded and they too were cast out. A new, more subservient computer arrived two days later but the moon and her light never returned.

Charlie grew fat. Opening the door to the fire escape to receive his pizza deliveries was the most effort he could make. The blinds remained shut and his spine arched until it mimicked the design of the chair. Sometimes he heard wind, rain, laughter, dogs barking but the twenty-first century still offered him nothing. The new computer was arrogant. It barely made a sound, unlike the wanton purring of The Slut. Its silence made Charlie paranoid, just like the sunshine did as it penetrated his darkened fort. When his back ached, Charlie would try to lie flat on the floor but the change in position made him nervous and throbbed his body until he wanted to cry so he remained in his chair instead. That way the arrogant machine could not second-guess him. *No-one would second-guess him again.*

Finally he found his nerve and with a great effort, launched the latest machine to its garden grave to join its predecessors. Months melded into years as Charlie grew fatter and developed a wheeze from the spores in the air that was left in the room. Bacteria spread into vile sores across his hunched body and his beard grew wide as well as long. Empty pizza boxes tiled the fortress floor and the rest of the house beneath began to rot from neglect. Machine after machine faded from his fickle affections and joined the other corpses in the graveyard at the bottom of the fire escape. Outside, so far away now it was unimaginable to Charlie, wars were declared and the earth struggled and burned but the twenty-first century still held no interest.

One day the pizza delivery company stopped coming. The fire escape was blocked with empty rotting cardboard and bits of old computer so they just stopped. The last man to attempt the climb stood for a few minutes in the garden and surveyed the incredible mountain of machinery that now grew there. Monitors, keyboards, external hard drives, scanners, speakers and forgotten memory clambered on top of each other, severed wires bled like cut veins from their bodies. *What a disgrace,* he thought and almost phoned the council.

Meanwhile, Charlie fought his virtual war with courage and discipline. He was a hero who led his men to victory through space, jungles, land mines and dangerous urban cityscapes. Finally he won, mere seconds before his virtual heart collapsed under the strain of his real body and he died.

Two months later, alerted by the vile stench, two men from the council collected his rotting remains. After clearing the fire escape and lifting the carcass clear from the old pizza boxes, they both paused at the site that greeted them beneath.

Bloody 'ell, said one of the men to the other, *look at that.* A shining mass of silver, fragile flowers covered the garden at the bottom of the fire escape, reflecting the sunlight in a metallic sheen of toxic wonder.

Beautiful.

Sally

This Christmastime

This Christmastime you'll join the world
Leaving the womb, at last uncurled

This Christmastime, you'll bring great joy
Little baby girl or baby boy

This Christmastime you'll learn to walk
And climb and play and laugh and talk

This Christmastime you'll be at school
Making new friends who'll think you're cool

This Christmastime you'll be a teen
Fuller of angst than you've ever been

This Christmastime you'll go to Uni
Drink too much and pull a moony

This Christmastime you'll go to work
Where problems abound and conflicts lurk

This Christmastime you'll find a spouse
Save some pennies, buy a house

This Christmastime you'll raise your own
Never again will you be alone

This Christmastime is your life of ease
Newly retired, you can do as you please

This Christmastime you'll leave this life
A soul transcending early strife

Jackie

May Auld Acquaintances Be Forgot

As the camera panned away from the fireworks showering over Big Ben, Margie launched herself from the sofa and switched off the television. The clock on the mantelpiece told her it was 12:04am. A sense of overwhelming relief poured through her body as the New Year images faded, she felt fresh and renewed, despite the boozy wooziness.

"Hey!" Dermot opened one eye accusingly, his body a collection of lumps under her best throw, "I was watching that!"

Disgusting, thought Margie as she wrenched the curtains open. The streetlights lit them all up like ugly decorations.

"What on earth...?" whined Dermot, shielding his eyes.

"Not now, Mum," groaned Kevin, wiping off Rosie's lip gloss and shoving his girlfriend's St Tropez limbs to one side. She tried to protest but lost her balance, knocking Dermot's ashtray over with her manicured hand - which created a minor explosion on the carpet. Kevin sighed and smashed down his beer can; his face the colour of a burnt sausage roll. But Margie recognised the sullen shadows spreading across his face and swiftly intercepted.

"Oh no. No. Don't even try to start whinging, Kevin." She puffed up her chest so violently that Dermot was briefly reminded of their honeymoon, thirty long years ago. Or was that from a film instead? He drained his dregs and closed his eyes again, trying to hide under his paper crown - oblivious to the silly string that decorated his bald patch.

"I've got an announcement to make." declared Margie. The full stop was so dramatic in this statement that continuing seemed t seemed futile. She gestured violently around the living room. "We live like a pack of claustrophobic sloths. I mean, just *look* at this place, look!"

Dutifully, they all looked. It seemed ok. There was a sofa, a couple of armchairs, a fireplace and a TV so large it almost formed a wall of its own. Everything was a sort of terracotta; a nod back to Margie's obsession with make-over shows during the 90s. There were scattered bottles, ashtrays, glasses, a couple of party-poppers and a collection of *Radio Times* stacked up high on the occasional table.

"Mum. You do this every year. There is nothing wrong with this room, the house or us. It's normal. We are normal. Get used to it. Put the telly back on, have another drink and shut up."

Speech over, Kevin sank back into the cushions with a victorious expression. Rosie giggled nervously, making all her bracelets jangle. Dermot snored.

But Margie had expected some form of apathetic rebellion from her brood of slugs. Power and tension formed an allegiance inside her chest and urged her onwards.

"It's *not* fine. This year will be different..."

To her annoyance she caught Kevin mouthing along with her sentence in perfect harmony. She flicked on all the lights, transforming the dingy room into an airport lounge. "So, from now on - no more television. We will go out at least twice a day for fresh air and wholesome, family activities. We shall play board-games every Sunday and have interesting debates over one of Nigella's roast dinners, which, by the way, will be served at the *table* and not on trays on our laps!"

Kevin raised his monobrow ever so slightly. "We don't have a table," he quipped smugly.

Rosie giggled again. Dermot opened an eye, lizard style, and glanced at her legs.

"Then we shall *buy* one." Margie's tone was dangerous.

"Oh shut up!" Kevin retorted. He reached under Rosie's skirt to find the remote, even though it was clearly lying on Dermot's lumpy stomach.

"Well, I'm entitled to some kind of life, even if the amoebas I'm surrounded by don't want one," bristled Margie.

She marched into the kitchen where three decades of frustration made her sweep all the dishes off the counter, bang the oven door so hard it fell off and throw eight glass tumblers straight out of the high cupboard. Feeling the glass and broken china scrunch so deliciously under her slippers ignited a pure rush of new energy and determination. Making as much noise and fuss as possible, she wrestled the hoover from its lair in the under stairs cupboard. Unleashing the hungry beast into the sloth-den in the lounge, she cackled and screamed,

"I should have done this *years* ago!" The hoover roared into action. Ash, hair, fluff, streamers and peanuts all flew happily up its nozzle.

"Mum! Stop it! Help, she needs sectioning!" yelled Kevin, jumping onto the occasional table as the hoover chased him. For once, Rosie did not giggle but dug her red talons into his arm instead, trying to reach safety.

Woman and vacuum continued their terrifying rampage through the terracotta sloth-cave. The hoover, imprisoned and starving for years, devoured cocktail umbrellas, balloons, toenails and sausage rolls, rugs and cushions, lights and socks and copies of the *Radio Times* and Rosie and Kevin and Dermot and....

Margie glanced at the clock above the mantelpiece. 12:34am. Only half an hour into the New Year and she'd never felt better.

And the living-room had never looked so tidy.

Sally

A Llama in Lima

 Howard groaned as his stomach twisted again. His eyes flickered open and rested on a huge pink llama. He squinted and focused again. A laugh came from the bed opposite him. "I guess that wasn't what you were expecting to see when you opened your eyes, was it, mate?" I reckon they shoved us both in the kiddies ward." The voice held an Australian twang.

Howard's gaze moved around the room to see walls generously decorated with posters of colourfully illustrated animals. In an alcove stood a simple wooden manger, holding straw and delicately carved figures. He looked across at his ward companion whose injuries looked fairly obvious from the cast on his leg. "I don't remember coming here. I was taking pictures...oh no, where the hell is my camera?"

The Australian inclined his head towards the cabinet and the camera that sat on the top of it. "You were out for the count when they brought you in, but you were still hanging onto that thing. Anyway, Merry Christmas, mate!"

144

Grimacing as another wave of pain hit him Howard wondered if he should ask for a bedpan or a sick bowl – and how to ask for either in Peruvian? Then, as the pain subsided, the stranger's words sunk in, and Howard asked "It's Christmas already?"

The man shrugged as his attention returned to the phone in his hand. "Maybe not for you, yet. You're a bit behind us, aren't you?"

Howard thought he sensed a dig in the comment somewhere and reached for his own phone which had been placed on the cabinet beside him. As usual he had no messages or missed calls – he was used to that – but he flicked quickly to Facebook to check for responses to his posts about his elaborate holiday. There were few, but one stood out. Laura had finally replied to his very first holiday post from four days ago. 'I hope you have a lovely time.' It was a simple reply (no kiss, he noted), and she hadn't commented on any subsequent posts. He wondered what Laura was doing and realised for the first time just how much he missed her. Howard closed his eyes and experienced more regret than he had ever felt before.

It had all come about when his accountancy firm had been amalgamated with a former rival company, and the subsequent dinner that had been held so they could get to know each other better. He had got to know one of their managers too well, and somehow it had got back to Laura. To his shock, she had ended their relationship and demanded he leave her flat immediately. He had expected her to calm down and relent, of course; after all, she had forgiven him just a couple of years back for a two-month affair, so why ruin things over such a minor indiscretion? As if a one-night stand with such a promiscuous lump of a woman could ever be a threat to their relationship? Had she not been 20 years younger than him, he wouldn't have looked twice, but it was always a notch on one's belt, wasn't it – a younger woman? Although that had been a disappointment too as it appeared she had propositioned a few of the older men in the firm before him, so he had actually looked more of a laughing stock than a stud – and the sex had been pretty rubbish too if he was honest.

He'd moved in temporarily with his brother who charged him an exorbitant amount of rent and ignored him most of the time. In his head, he'd imagined leading a lively bachelor life full of nights out with the boys which would make Laura think again, but it transpired he didn't have any boys who wanted to go out with him and he soon had to admit to feeling very lonely.

Initially Laura's stubbornness perplexed him; and he found himself stalking her social media to find that she was re-connecting with old friends and enjoying life far more then he was. He came to the conclusion he had to do something drastic to make her see what she was missing. One wet and miserable November night from the discomfort of his drab bedroom, he came up with the answer. He would book a luxury holiday for over Christmas. His brother had already dropped very heavy hints that they had friends coming for Christmas and would be short of space – on bedrooms and table space, apparently – so how better to kill two birds with one stone?

The idea had taken wings and grown. Laura had talked endlessly about wanting to see llamas in the wild. She was obsessed with llamas and wanted to do the fancy treks in Peru, so where better to go than the place she dreamed about. Of course, he had no intention of doing any trekking – no way, Jose, that was far too energetic for him. No, he had opted for a for a nice warm beach holiday at a 5* hotel in Lima which had cost him an absolute fortune, but he saw it as an investment in his future. He had booked it through a solo traveller's company and had paid for a couple of trips to be thrown in for good measure. He saw the photo opportunities as being endless, and intended to share them far and wide on social media to show Laura he was living her dream. He figured there must be llamas around somewhere nearby – after all, Peru was Peru, wasn't it?

It had all started quite well. They were a reasonable bunch, his fellow solo travellers, and

148

he had managed to persuade a couple of the better-looking women among them to have their photos taken with him. He didn't particularly gel with many of them and found several of the men quite overbearing and critical. But the hotel was luxurious, the all-inclusive food and drink seemed never-ending and the sea was warm. He spent his first couple of days eating, drinking and sun-bathing to his heart's content, and began to relax, despite the constant underlying pang that he wished Laura was there with him.

It was on day three that it all unravelled. The temperature in Peru had increased and it was the day he had booked to take a tour inland to a traditional Peruvian village for a meal and entertainment. It also included enough walking to look like a trek in pictures. He woke feeling bloated, burnt and bitten. Laura had always ensured they had plenty of sunscreen and insect repellent and had a big bag of pills, potions and plasters. He had failed miserably in his packing. He considered cancelling the trip, but doubted he'd get his money back, and besides, this would probably be his best chance of getting llama pictures – they were bound to have some in the villages.

The air-conditioned minibus felt like heaven but he still felt out of sorts. He sat next to the good-looking one whose name was Thelma. He couldn't take her seriously after she'd told him her name, it always made him think of Scooby Doo, but she would look good in his photos and so he manoeuvred her into the window seat to casually catch her image on photos he took from the bus.

The guide's voice droned on during the journey and Howard closed his eyes to sleep, but a pounding headache began to develop behind his right temple. "Do you have any paracetamol?" he asked Thelma. She did and gave him two along with a bottle of water from her bag – a little begrudgingly though, he thought.

As they came to the outskirts of the village, the minibus slowed and children came out, many dressed in Peruvian national dress, their faces bright and smiling under their colourful woolly hats and scarves. They waved happily to the passengers, and Howard enthusiastically snapped away, despite his annoyance at the seeming lack of llamas. "They can go and change back into their designer jeans now." Howard remarked sarcastically once he'd got his photos. "Bet their parents get paid well for that little appearance." Thelma tutted and turned away.

The minibus parked, and they were ushered into a large, ornate hall where tables were laid simply with pristine white tablecloths. They were all seated and offered wine or beer. Howard's head was thumping now and he didn't want to ask Thelma for more paracetamol, so he ordered beer and hoped for the best. They all trooped up for the buffet, Howard watching anxiously as two of the men from his group helped themselves to huge portions of the meat stew that seemed to be the highpoint of the buffet, while he was still stuck near the back of the queue. He quickly bypassed a couple of older women who were clearly dithering and when he reached the tureen, ladled as much stew onto his plate at it would hold, wincing at the dull thump behind his brow as he carried the plateful back to his seat. Using his napkin, he wiped the sweat on his neck away. The stew turned out to be as fiery as hell and Howard gulped at his beer, ordering two more pints – well, it was all free! The waiter looked about to argue, but Howard scowled and laid his cutlery down noisily, and the boy backed down.

By the time the entertainment began, Howard was feeling decidedly sick and unsteady but he was determined to get snaps of it – Laura would be gagging at these, though he doubted they'd have any performing llamas. There were however more of those sweet -looking children dancing and then another bunch singing. He tried to steady his camera, but his hand was shaking and his vision became blurred. His stomach churned and he began to gasp for breath...

"Mr Staines?" Howard looked up from his phone to see a short dark-skinned man, smartly dressed in a flannel suit and open-necked shirt, had entered his hospital room. "I am Mr Molinero, the on-duty consultant. I've spoken to the doctors who examined you and looked at your test results."

"Yes." Howard looked up at him. "Have you found out what's wrong with me?" Howard had gone over this in his head briefly and imagined dysentery or food poisoning were the most likely cause. He had a solicitor friend who would be all over it – he reckoned he might get another holiday out of it.

"I'm pleased to tell you there is nothing major wrong. We will be releasing you later today." Howard opened his mouth to complain but the consultant beat him to it. "You had quite a serious case of sunstroke and several nasty mosquito bites for which we will give you antibiotic ointment to use. Your condition has been exacerbated by an excessive intake of spicy food and alcohol. You need to be sensible about your sun, food and drink intake here, even if it is free." The man pulled no punches, but he did it in perfect English. "However, there are signs you may have an existing stomach ulcer, which you should get checked out when you return home"

"But there must have been something wrong with the food." Howard's voice was feeble.

The consultant shook his head. "The only thing wrong with the food was the quantity you probably ate. Now, is there anyone we can call to collect you?"

Howard's phone beeped in his hand and a picture of Laura apparently having the time of her life at a Christmas party appeared. Out of the corner of his eye, it seemed as though the big pink llama was laughing at him. "No." he said miserably, knowing there was only one person he wanted to pick him up and he had lost her forever.

Jackie

Christmas Quiz Answers

1. David Tennant

2. Peter Capaldi

3. The Office

4. Eight

5. An angel gets its wings

6. Catherine Tate

7. Treat Every Day Like Christmas

8. Blue

9. You Send Me By Aretha Franklin

10. Los Angeles

Printed in Great Britain
by Amazon